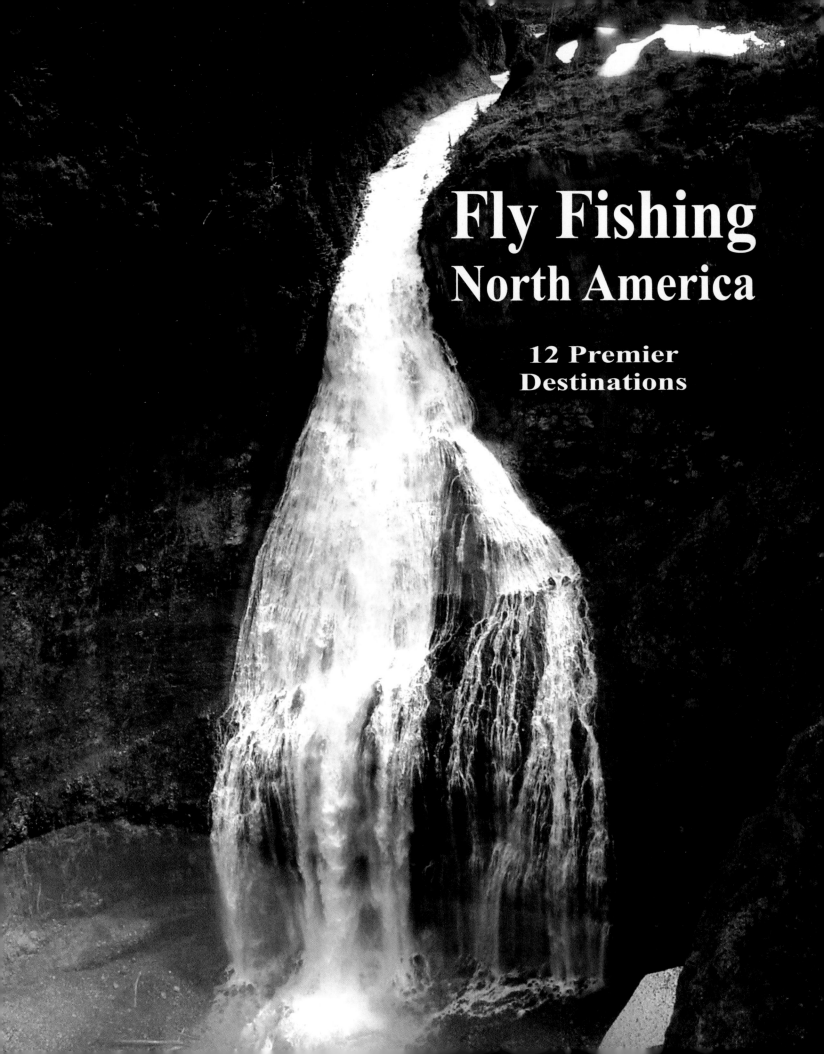

Fly Fishing
North America

12 Premier Destinations

AUTHORS: David B. Mouser and Louis Perella

EDITORS: Barbara Brannon, Joe Crowder

PHOTOGRAPHY: Louis Perella, David Mouser, South Carolina; Drake Whitlock, North Carolina; Steve Davis, Nimmo Bay, British Columbia; Don Muelrath, California; Brett Mouser, Colorado; AnneReb, North Carolina

COVER PHOTOGRAPHY: Don Muelrath, California

CORPORATE: Tom Rosenbauer, Orvis Company

Cataloging-in-Publications Data
Library of Congress Control Number: 2002114142

Mouser, Perella, (David Mouser, Louis Perella)
1. H. P. Publishing, Ltd (U. S.) I. Title copyright

ISBN 1-929771-11-8
© Copyright 2003 H. P. Publishing, Ltd.

FIRST EDITION
10 9 8 7 6 5 4 3 2 1

Contents

* Orvis Endorsed Lodge

Introduction

William Shakespeare was an avid student of fly fishing during his youth. George Catlin, the famous Northwest adventurer, in his trek up the Missouri Breaks in 1833, found the trout of North America to be quite distinctive. Often fearsome in their feeding frenzies, trout rose to what George Catlin described as the "snow flake-like" hatches of thousands of bugs breaking water in the mountain streams. Teddy Roosevelt loved to fish the Brule River in northern Wisconsin at the early 1900s. The fall river runs of the steelhead, brown trout, and rainbow trout were his favorites. Charles Kuralt, 20th-century icon and commentator, immortalized fly fishing when Bob Timberlake, a wonderful outdoor artist from North Carolina, painted *Kuralt at White's Creek* (an oil painting dedicated to Bob's dear friend shortly after Kuralt's death). These are but a handful of the notable ambassadors of the great outdoor sport of fly fishing.

As for the rest of us, don't despair. We are well represented by a longtime champion of the common man, Walter Mitty. In the *New Yorker* magazine Walter Mitty was always our ambassador . . . his daydreams of being the immortal Babe Ruth or the Olympic Gold Medal Champion were our dreams too. Walter taught us we can all be in the World Series - and of course be the star!

But wait a minute: we don't need Walter Mitty or daydreams for fly fishing; anyone can slip down into the cool waters of a mountain stream, wade quietly through crystal-clear water, and enjoy the wonderful experience of fly fishing. And if you need some daydreams, who is to say that William, Teddy and Charles aren't waiting for us just around the bend. I often do some of my best daydreaming when I am in the stream.

Our streams and fisheries are all very special, and in a way, we all share them equally. They are all the same in one respect: no matter where we go, the one common denominator is time - the "time" that always disappears and remains fleeting as we shoot our lines in a graceful arc of timeless majesty. "I can't believe it's time to leave. What happened to my day? Oh well, what a great day!"

Fly fishing is an art, but not in casting, nor in angling ability or even in successfully netting a trout. Many, many books have been written on the subject. They expound on casting, holding the rod, and other technical matters. The art is a one-on-one personal experience. The stream is your personal canvas; your paintbrush is the eight-to ten-foot rod moving through the air, and the art - well it's something different to each of us. Art is the "beauty" in the eye of the beholder. I like to think that when I make that final presentation of my fly upon the water, similar to the moment the artist's brush touches the canvas, my spirit touches the top of the water at exactly the same time.

Opposite: *A remote waterfall in North America (we're keeping it a secret) that empties into a beautiful gin-clear fishing hole where we found the trophies that bent our rods to the max*

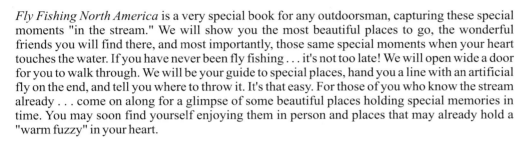

Fly Fishing North America is a very special book for any outdoorsman, capturing these special moments "in the stream." We will show you the most beautiful places to go, the wonderful friends you will find there, and most importantly, those same special moments when your heart touches the water. If you have never been fly fishing . . . it's not too late! We will open wide a door for you to walk through. We will be your guide to special places, hand you a line with an artificial fly on the end, and tell you where to throw it. It's that easy. For those of you who know the stream already . . . come on along for a glimpse of some beautiful places holding special memories in time. You may soon find yourself enjoying them in person and places that may already hold a "warm fuzzy" in your heart.

Fly Fishing North America is a beautiful pictorial essay of the top twelve fly fishing destinations across North America. Each lodge and destination represents a different outdoor experience. You will find different species of trout and salmon, pristine streams and lakes, views of rustic and warm accommodations in remote wilderness regions, and most important, the people who live in the midst of this beauty every day.

They are a special breed of people dedicated to the outdoors. There are the Libbys, who represent over 110 years in the fly fishing business in the remote wilderness of Northern Maine; Kirk Gay (son of Ward Gay his father, early Alaskan bush pilot and outdoor adventurer) and his wife, Liza, of Alaska's Valhalla Lodge; John and Mary Lou Blackwell of Moose Lake Lodge, who pioneered the wilds of central British Columbia and raised their two young children there; Craig and Deborah Murray, who created Nimmo Bay's Heli-Venture (the ultimate in fly fishing, using helicopters as you would a raft in the stream), along with their sons and daughter in a remote wilderness of Western Canada. They all share a common thread: an exciting and remote lifestyle located in the forests and wilderness regions of North America.

All of the destinations featured provide a pristine adventure into the great outdoors. They are equal in every respect to the qualities of the stream, each lodge or resort evoking a warm spirit of friendship and camaraderie. Their happiness is simply your visit into their world. All of these premier locations represent unique families dedicated to fly-fishing adventures. Many are third- and fourth-generation anglers, a fact that speaks for itself.

In writing this guide, we were looking for a warm spirit of camaraderie in addition to full lodging and food services. Family and tradition were basic requirements. Our main focus was to find and document the best fly fishing in each geographic location, with emphasis upon the species, the outdoor environment or location, and the element of adventure. From an exotic stream lunch by helicopter on a 9,000-foot glacier in British Columbia to a simple lunchbox meal on the Big East Fork of the Pigeon River in a pristine Southern Appalachian forest in North Carolina, we found each adventure to be unique and rewarding.

We do not mean to portray that these twelve are the only destinations of their caliber, nor have we purposely ignored saltwater fly fishing. Our primary focus is freshwater fly fishing for great North American fish. Geography was an important consideration, as we chose these destinations to represent a cross section of the great fisheries in continental North America. More important, they represent the premier destinations to fish each species: rainbow, cutthroat, browns, grayling, brook, steelheads, and Pacific salmon are but a few.

We personally visited each lodge or resort and experienced firsthand the facilities, fisheries, guides, and services each one offered. Each provided an exhilarating adventure. We sought to share accounts of these adventures with readers in addition to providing a pictorial representation of what it is like to visit each destination. Welcome to *Fly Fishing North America.*

Grab a rod, get ready to travel, and let's go fishing!

Opposite: *One of the many Bighorn River browns that average 16" to 18" with a few 22" & 24" "lunkers" cruising in the shallows.*

Dry Falls in North Carolina

Foreward

Kuralt at White's Creek   by Bob Timberlake

"Shall I go
to heaven . . . or shall I go fishing?"

Fortunately for me, Charles Kuralt and I spent many wonderful hours together talking about what we loved most and what meant the most to us in life. We talked about times past . . . "when folks lived farther apart, yet closer together."

We also talked about fishing. Both of us loved to fish, especially for trout, catching one or two now and again. Charles told me that it's not catching the fish that's important . . . .it's being there.

Charles was always at peace on a trout stream, more than at any other place. One of the very last things I said to him while he was in the hospital in New York just before his death was, "I'll get you back home here in North Carolina and we'll go to the mountains and fish." I realized how very ill he was when he responded,

> *"Was it Thoreau who said, Shall I go to heaven . . . or shall I go fishing?"'*

I really believe Charles is fishing on a sparkling cold mountain stream up in heaven at this very moment. I hope he is. Just being there with a good friend or a big brown hiding under a Rock . . . it's what we love and, hopefully, what we can pass on.

Bob Timberlake

Alaska

Valhalla Lodge

Captain Kirk Gay and his wife Liza

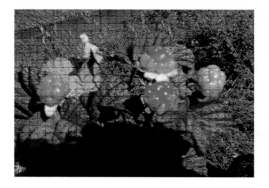

Valhalla, in the land of the midnight sun, is truly the wilderness experience located on Six Mile Lake, 187 miles SW of Anchorage by air. Captain Kirk Gay and his wife Liza, along with his son Chris, daughter Brenda and his son-in-law Brad, represent a dynasty in outdoor fly fishing and Alaskan hospitality. Valhalla dates back to 1935, when Ward Gay first settled in Alaska. Kirk's father Ward, is a legend in Alaska and flew thousands of hours in the de Haviland Beaver floatplane. It is still used extensively today to fly Valhalla guests to the remote regions of the Iliamna region.

Above: *Sunrise in the land of the midnight sun. Each day is a fly out to a new location.*

Middle: *A view of Valhalla's lakefront cabins and lodge.*

Bottom: *The natural beauty of the Alaskan outdoors is reflected in the Salmon Berry and the Alaskan Lilac.*

Left: *Lodge facilities and recreation, lodge bedroom in one of the cabins on Six Mile Lake.*

Below *Rare Alaska lynx decorate the interior of the warm and cozy lodge.*

Above: *The lodge is a cozy gathering place each evening where stories of the day are shared among the guests.*

"Ooooops!"

Above: *Drake Whitlock, from North Carolina, and coauthor David Mouser share many doubles, and in the picture above, it is all they can do to hold these salmon for a picture . . . "Oops there goes another one . . .back in the stream!"   We finally have a picture of the "one that truly got away"*

Our July visit, provided chum salmon, trout and grayling adventures worth a lifetime. The rustic lodge and charm of the cabins were second only to the dinners prepared by Chef Cookie.

Sunrise and sunset were ever spectacular and the days in mid-summer lasted forever. The sunset was 11:35 each evening with the twilight of morning and afternoon lasting what seemed like forever. Four to five hours of darkness each day is a little unusual if you are not accustomed to this latitude.

A small hatch just at sunset off our front porch on the edge of the lake, produced lots of activity and we caught our first fish, a beautiful grayling. We were testing a new rod and we did not want to miss the opportunity to target one of those top water swirls.

Valhalla is truly a paradise for outdoorsman. The lodge consists of 6 cabins (double beds) overlooking beautiful Six Mile Lake. Valhalla's fleet of floatplanes fly their guests out to the wilds of Alaska each day. Fly fishing in the world famous Iliamna region of Alaska is a dream come true. Besides the trophy Pacific salmon and the Alaskan rainbows, we found an abundance of grayling. (Almost non existent in many areas of the lower 48) And needless to say, all are "big" in Alaska.

Valhalla is reached by floatplane and in turn they fly their guests from the lodge to remote glacier lakes, to the coast for fresh run Pacific salmon and rainbows, and to the mountains and throughout the tundra to pristine and secret fisheries known only by their pilot guides. Ward Gay was one of the early pioneer in early Alaska, flying thousands of miles for pleasure, exploration and big game hunting expeditions. Capt. Kirk Gay and his family continue the traditions that his father Ward began so many years ago. It is centered around the love for the awesome outdoors of Alaska and providing thrilling adventures into the interior of Alaska in search of trophy fish and game. Their flying program to remote areas combines over 100 years of experience in the great outdoors of Alaska, truly one of the exotic lodges in the land of the midnight sun!

Above: *Each morning our pilot-guide Brad Waitman, radioed in for a weather report to determine what areas in the Alaskan wilderness were accessible for that day's fishing. Often the other pilot-guides in the area would pass on great fishing information which was a courtesy extended between all of the bush pilots we later learned.*

Our pilot guide, Capt. Kirk's son-in-law Brad Waitman, flew us out to a secret spring-fed lake on the Alaskan tundra to begin our first day. These wild native rainbows were stacked solid and that meant non-stop fly fishing from morning until we said, "uncle."

Chums, a variety of Pacific salmon, highlighted our second day on a fly out to the Aukia River. Every other cast was non-stop action, averaging eight to twelve pounds which kept us busy from the time we landed in the river until our return to the lodge. Sand bars in the middle of the streams provide excellent floatplane anchorage and every fishing destination was presented to us on a twenty pound test leader and eight weight sinking tip lines. Salmon strike out of aggravation and habit as they seldom feed during their migrations up the rivers and streams to their ancestral spawning grounds.

Alaska's Secret Treasure: Grayling

Opposite page: *The solitude of the stream and the beauty of the wilderness, accelerate the experiences of fly fishing in Alaska. It's a land of wild adventure. Always be prepared to see a few of Alaska's native residents - the bears!*

Left: *One of the many grayling we caught on the last day of our adventure at a hole known as "the aquarium." Drake Whitlock displays one of the "average size" (trophy in my book) graylings.*

Below: *A beautiful coho salmon on your fly rod is a battle and a memory for a long time to come.*

An hour's flight from the lodge, nestled high in the mountains, lies a pristine, deep-blue water, spring-fed lake we chose to call Mirror Lake. We landed early in the morning, and after getting our gear in order, we walked approximately a mile up the small stream to a secluded bend where we found the aquarium hole, a huge crystal-clear fishing hole about ten feet deep.

We observed a lot of top water activity and quickly tied on everything from Royal Wolffs to Parachute Adams. They all worked . . . the grayling were feeding on a pale morning dun hatch that seemed to be in pockets in all directions. The Alaskan grayling is abundant in the higher elevations. Grayling require a very cold temperature usually 52 to 55 degrees and clear water is a must for these almost rare fish. Their size averaged twelve to sixteen inches and we thoroughly enjoyed almost non-stop action that lasted well past our stream lunch and into mid-afternoon.

We reluctantly left this hidden spot as we needed the extra time in late afternoon to return to the floatplane and fly back to the lodge. Brad Waitman, our pilot-guide was extremely knowledgeable not only in fly fishing techniques but truly a great outdoorsman and wonderful pilot. It takes a special breed of man to live in this wilderness and we often thought that Brad was actually part of the land. As we completed our day, a huge bull moose plunged into the water to begin his afternoon meal of aquatic plant life and vegetation. Fly fishing in Alaska is a multitude of turn-ons . . . plenty of fish, wonderful landscapes, and a great feeling of being truly alive in the clean environ of Alaska's wilderness.

Special names like Yellow Mountain, Blow Hole, Sugar Loaf Mountain, Kijik River will always be special to me as I remember the outdoor adventures provided each day by the wonderful guides of Valhalla Lodge. Alaska is truly the land of the midnight sun and I found it to be twice as exciting as what I had anticipated.

Above: *Floatplanes not only provide transportation to the fish, they also give you a glimpse of some of the most picturesque remote regions where the natural environment is still unspoiled..*

Right: *Guide Brad Waitman helps a Valhalla guest get rigged up for a remote fishing adventure high in one of Alaska's glacier lakes.*

Valhalla Lodge, Summer 2002
Score: Angler 1, Fish 0
"Alaska on a fly rod is the ultimate fly fishing adventure!"

British Columbia

Moose Lake Lodge
British Columbia

Above: *The new commercial air strip to Moose Lake Lodge is unique for a remote and isolated wilderness location. Flights are scheduled one day each week, providing guests with comfortable flights direct from Vancouver. Everyday access to the lodge is provided by floatplanes from Anaheim Lake. Moose Lake Lodge is in the background.*

Moose Lake Lodge is three hundred miles north of Vancouver, smack-dab in the middle of British Columbia's pristine wilderness. Bald eagles fish with you every day in addition to moose, black bears, grizzly bears, caribou, elk, beavers, and native wild Canada geese to complete a wonderful outdoor experience. Add to this wild rainbows, cutthroat, salmon, and trophy steelhead, and you're set for some serious fly fishing!

The remote setting is Moose Lake, a wilderness forest ringed by snow-capped glacier mountains, the Black Water River, the Upper Dean River, and the Lower Dean River (famous for its summer-run fresh steelheads and the Blackwell family who will make your visit a memorable event). All of British Columbia's fish require plenty of line and plenty of backing.

Top Right: *Moose Lake Lodge accommodates a maximum of eighteen anglers in eight private cabins offering full services, wonderful food, and some of Canada's finest guides.*

Above: *The lodge dining provides a spectacular view of Moose Lake. Chef Bernie is the key to the wonderful dining experience. And . . . the stream lunches (packed with your guide) are "to die for" after a hearty morning in the stream.*

The lodge is accessible only by air. With the addition of the new grass strip beside the lodge, private planes now have access, and a Saturday flight direct from Vancouver has been initiated (approximate flight time is one and a half hours by turbojet). The main lodge contains a huge great room, built from hand-hewn logs timbered from the Blackwell property. John and Mary Lou Blackwell pioneered Moose Lake some thirty-five years ago, bringing their sons, seven-year-old son Justin and five-year-old Sid, to this wilderness paradise with the hopes of forging a hunting and fishing lodge in the wilderness.

Today Sid is one of the lodge's chief pilots, flying guests to remote fishing lakes and streams in dependable de Havilland Beaver floatplanes. Justin is part owner and manager of the legendary Moose Lake Dean River Camp.

Above: *Moose Lake Lodge guest, Beau Purvis, lands a beautiful steelhead on the Dean in British Columbia. The Dean River Lodge, fishes the first two miles of the Dean, fishes by permit. All of the fresh run "chromers" are a highlight for Moose Lake anglers.*

Fishing for Steelhead on the Dean

The legendary Dean River is noted for it's beautiful "chromers," fresh ocean run wild steelheads that will send your reel spinning. A thirty mile stretch beginning at Moose Lake's Dean River Lodge is catch and release - fly only. A limited season extends from June 15 to August 15 for steelhead. The camp opens again for the Coho and Sockeye salmon runs in September.

The Dean River Lodge, just like the Moose Lake Lodge is accessible only by plane. (Flying time from Moose lake is approximately 45 minutes) The wide open areas affords not only easy access for fishing the runs and pools but also provides an ideal environment for flying with a 14' spey rod. The effortless ease in casting is equaled by the beauty and arch of the spey rod's casting pattern. And of course, once you hook up one of the steelheads from the Dean, you are in for a real treat. Imagine a freight train on the end of your fly rod that is moving like lightning and all you can hear is the whine of your reel as all of your backing disappears! I saw a seasoned steelheader fight a trophy steelhead for over 45 minutes. We estimated after he landed him, he was every bit of 18 lbs! You don't catch every one . . . that's for sure! *What's so special about the legendary Dean River in British Columbia?* For a starter the steelhead run occurs in the summer months (June 15 - August 15) which means warm weather fishing, sunshine, ideal temperatures and long days unlike the spring and fall seasons which often incur cold and damp weather in the other fisheries of North America.

The demographics of the Dean River allows easy wading in addition to spacious access over the water for casting and the use of 14' spey rods. Numerous runs and pools are abundant throughout the 30 mile fly (catch & release section). The icing on the cake is the location; beautiful British Columbia complete with glaciers, waterfalls and remote wilderness. (between Tweedsmuir and Kitlope Provincial Parks). This is an awesome wilderness and wildlife refuge accessed only by floatplane or boat for 60 miles in any direction. And to place a "lock" on it consider that the angling permits are very limited so that your only competition are the bald eagles and the bears as they fatten themselves for winter on the spawning fish. This also protects the fishery from being over-worked. The lower Dean River in British Columbia is "steelhead heaven!"

Above and Left: The de Haviland Beaver floatplane buzzes the angles on the Blackwater River as he leaves for home. We found this river to be one of the most beautiful fisheries in British Columbia, teeming with wild rainbows. It is some of the best dry fly fishing for wild native rainbows in North America. The fly out is 45 minutes by floatplane which lands in the middle of the river for ingress and egress. It is pure wilderness!

These rainbows feed aggressively as they are in competition with "squaw fish" which accelerates their need for survival and both are well balanced in this wild fishery. They are trained for "combat" from the beginning and transfer this zeal to your fly rod when you are hooked up with this special breed. Every bend and run in the river is filled with rainbows from 12 to 16 inches. Your only real competition is the American Bald Eagle and the Golden Eagle. They occasionally swoop down and grab a rainbow from the surface water.

Left: *Stream flowers*   Center: *A rest break as we float to the next run*   Right: *A welcome break - stream lunch on the Blackwater.*

Fly fishing the Black Water was one of the most memorable streams we fished in British Columbia. The natural beauty of the wild flowers blooming at the end of July, the cool morning temperatures changing to shirt sleeves by noon, the friendship and comradery of floating the stream, getting out occasionally to fish the runs and deep pools, the stream lunch where the patterns of the day were discussed and how "the big one got away", is what I call "The Black Water River total package!"

Top: *Every day is a fly out to remote streams and lakes to fish.*

Above left: *Coauthor David Mouser lands a nice pink salmon*

Above Center: *Lodge owner John Blackwell, coauthor Lou Perella and Drake Whitlock all take credit for a nice coho salmon.*

Above Right: *Guide Justin Blackwell, the owner's oldest son, rows coauthor Lou Perella back to the plane. In the background, pilot Sid Blackwell, the owner's youngest son, prepares for the return flight to the lodge.*

Everyday is a
Flyout!

Left: Moose Lake Lodge owners John and Mary Lou Blackwell pose for a picture with coauthor David Mouser and Drake Whitlock of North Carolina, as they send them off on another day's adventure in the remote British Columbia wilderness.

Below: The de Haviland Beaver floatplane provides quick and easy access to the remote and secret fisheries that owner John Blackwell has pioneered for the past 25 years.

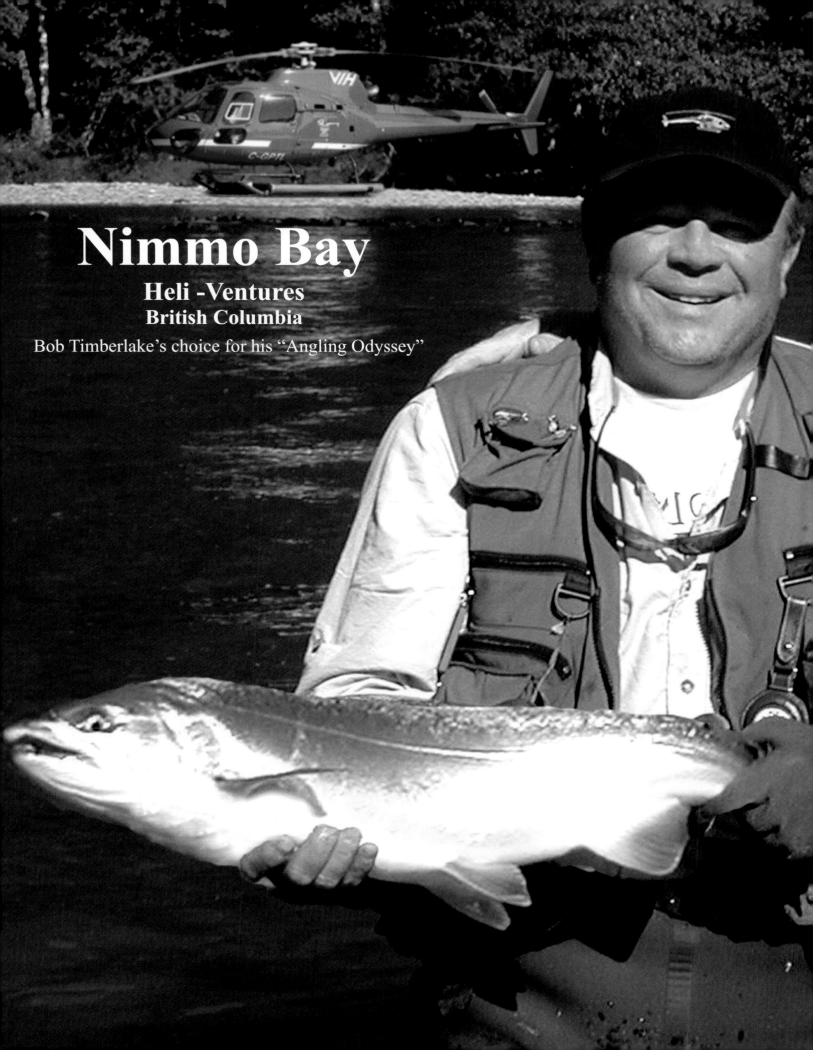

Nimmo Bay

Heli -Ventures
British Columbia

Bob Timberlake's choice for his "Angling Odyssey"

Craig Murray and Bob Timberlake with a nice fresh run Silver salmon

$$E^2 = MC^{™}$$

Theory of Hospitality

"Expectations Exceeded = Memories Created"

Aerial View of Nimmo Bay
(waterfront cabins)

Waterfront cabins, the staff waving "hello," guest arrival by helicopter, "welcome everyone"
evening cocktail hour, dinner gathering of guests, an after-dinner guitar sing,
hot tub overlooking waterfall, living room, native flower, bedroom

Nimmo Bay is located in the central coastal area of British
Columbia approximately one hour from Vancouver. It is a
theater in the wilderness and it functions whenever people
are present. The encore is each new day!

Top: *Top of a glacier known as "The Hand of God"*

Above right: *Coauthor David Mouser and Nimmo Bay owner Craig Murray share special time together on the mountain top*

Left: *The Lee Brandsma family from Chicago; Josh, Pamela, Ryan, Emily and Lee pose with a ten thousand year old glacier in the background. To their left is a beautiful rock coloration of diversified mineral deposits.*

Imagine being able to move from stream to stream and go where the fish are and visit streams that only the bears can get to . . . "Heli Fish" is Nimmo's term for helicopter access. Each guest is assigned to one of Nimmo Bay's A Star B-2 helicopters, providing comfortable seating for 6 adults plus your pilot (fishing guide). As they say at Nimmo Bay, "To Fly is Human . . . To Hover, Divine"

And fun . . . ? Well, try flying out each morning to a remote and secret stream or glacier fed lake to begin a real adventure into the outdoors. The heart of fishing in this wilderness is concentrated on trophy Pacific salmon (all species) with some great cutthroats for dessert.

Our first day we fished a remote wilderness stream filled with beautiful Pink salmon. We used 6 wt. fly rods to fish these 6 to 8 pound beauties. All fishing is barbless, full release. The morning was filled with fish after fish. I thought the adventure was well under way but when noon approached, we jumped back in the A Star helicopter and 7,000 feet later we were enjoying lunch on top of a ten-thousand-year old glacier. Full linen, a selection of red and white wines and a delicious lunch were prepared by the Nimmo Bay Chefs sparing no creativity. Absolutely delicious! After the lunch break we jumped in the copter and back to the stream for an afternoon of great fly fishing! And the ones that got away? Well, I must admit I really never missed them as we had more than our share!

Left: *One of British Columbia's magnificent waterfalls as viewed from our helicopter.*
Top: *Deborah Murray shows how easy it is to enjoy a waterfall with a fly rod in hand*
Above: *Jane Pritchett and pilot-guide Duncan Patrick discuss the CD music to play on our stereo head phones during flight*
Right: *Coauthor Lou Perella nets a beautiful fresh run Pacific Pink salmon*

We found Nimmo Bay to be a "fly" fishing experience extraordinare! It is the "Champagne and Caviar" of angling in the wilderness. Their fishery is catch and release using barbless hooks.

Each day was an adventure planned around fly fishing. The helicopters not only provide access but they serve as "windows into the fisheries." The ability to hover over "gin clear" water and spot the concentrations of fish, was certainly a huge asset. The three cardinal rules of fly fishing, *"go where there are fish, stay with the fish and watch your fly."*

Going where there are fish is a given by helicopter, staying with the fish is hard to do when it's time to "heli" out to a mountain glacier or pristine waterfall for lunch. Of course, you are going back to a different spot, usually loaded with more "lunkers" after lunch . . . I guess watching your fly is the most difficult rule to remember. The awesome beauty of the surrounding scenery imposingly demands your attention.

Top: *A ten-thousand-year-old glacier flowing to the sea* Above left: *Guest Jane Pritchett of New York with a fresh-run pink salmon displayed by owner Craig Murray* Above center: *Another of British Columbia's fabulous living glaciers* Above right: *The solitude of British Columbia is as beautiful as the blue of the stream.*

Nimmo Bay actually is a three-stage family destination: the immediate family, the extended family, and the corporate family. Whether you are seeking a fly-fishing adventure, traveling with your immediate family of spouse and children, or entertaining corporate clients or personnel, Nimmo Bay is the exotic "champagne" destination of fly fishing. In just four days we explored over thirty thousand square miles of wilderness, shared great adventures with families in all three categories, and never found anything to be other than great camaraderie among a group of people who reach for perfection! Nimmo Bay's success is centered on humor and a detailed presentation of fly fishing by helicopter and music. The owners, Craig and Deborah Murray, along with their talented family members Steve, Fraser, Clifton, and Georgia, occasionally provide entertainment with their guitars following dinner.

Nimmo Bay
Heli - Ventures

Yukon

British Columbia

Nimmo Bay

Alberta

Vancouver

Victoria

A Pristine Land of Dreams
"where the spirit of life dwells . . .
that's where you want to be"

We were looking for that special vacation in a world centered around fly fishing and we found it. Nimmo Bay provides more than your expectations. Their E^2 theory of hospitality is very simple . . .

Expectations Exceeded = Memories Created (E^2 = MC) TM

They do just that! Bob Timberlake quoted the late Charles Kuralt in his forward of *Fly Fishing North America* as saying, 'Shall I go to heaven . . . or shall I go fishing?' For those of you that want to kick fly fishing up a notch with family and friends, you may say, "Is it time to go fly fishing . . . or is it time to go on a Fly Fishing Heli - Venture?"

Left: *Lunch on top of a glacier is not only exotic but fun*

Above: *The Nimmo Bay helicopters blend fly fishing with the ultimate in adventure!*

49

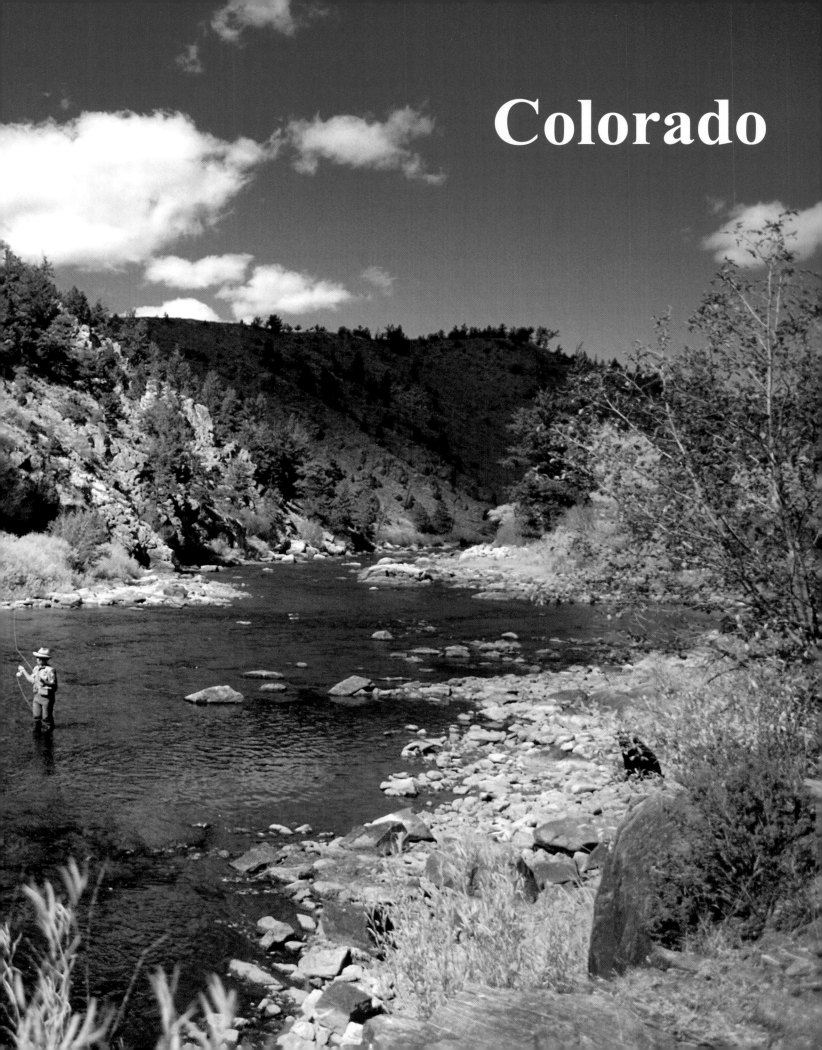

Colorado

Above: *Broadacres guide with a happy guest and a wild rainbow trout from the Rio Grande River*

Left: *Broadacres Ranch is 4.5 miles just outside the old silver mining town of Creede, Colorado (famous during the silver rush of 1892). Shallow Creek provides pocket-water-pools of browns and rainbows. Two miles of the Rio Grande wind lazily through the ranch providing wild rainbows and browns reaching twenty inches in size.*

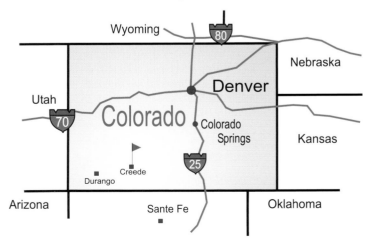

Above: *The Rio Grande is teeming with wild rainbow and brown trout.*   Opposite bottom: *The landscape and beauty of Broadacres Ranch are unequaled in splendor and majesty.*

Broadacres owner Charles Nearburg is a fundamentalist in his approach to improving the stream condition in both fisheries, with extensive modification of the "bio-structures" and hydraulics of each, thus providing an improved habitat for trout species and angler alike. Additional feeding troughs and deep-water stream pools were created by replacing some 1,500 boulders in strategic locations in the Rio Grande and Shallow Creek. The results are two "diamonds" to explore and fish. Shallow Creek is a wonderfully selective fishing experience and, we believe, one of the ultimate fisheries in pocket-water "sight fishing" for trophy rainbows and browns. The cold spring-fed waters from the mountains, in addition to the foliage, maintain a cool water temperature for excellent fishing. The oxygen levels are increased by the gentle flowing falls from one pool to the other. Shallow Creek is "tight" like a champion golf course, requiring different skills and techniques. The Broadacres guides are willing and able to teach you the "secrets" of Shallow Creek!

On the first day our warm-up began at Glenmora Lake (Shallow Creek's final destination and part of eleven acres of trophy lakes at Broadacres). By day two, we were fishing the Rio Grande each morning about ten, as a caddis hatch was almost ever-present each morning. Lou experienced a huge hatch by 10:30, and he quit counting after about twenty rainbows in the hour and a half that it lasted. Just ¼ mile up stream we had a few PMD's (pale morning duns) and a few caddis on the water. I was catching 16- to 18-inch browns and rainbows, totaling seven in all, during the same time coauthor Lou Perella was trying to "breathe" in the caddis hatch.

The exciting loss was a cast that fell behind a huge boulder in midstream. Almost immediately there was a huge explosion of water behind the rock. I was totally unprepared to set the hook, as I anticipated pulling it over the rock and dropping it just in front (which worked on the third cast at the same target, netting a beautiful 18-inch rainbow). We were able to easily wade upstream in the Rio Grande, stalking each bubble line in the pools and feeding troughs that we encountered. Every ten to fifteen minutes provided an exciting fight on my 5-wt. rod (mid-flex), which reflected wonderful rod action on this size fish. Pale morning duns, caddis, green drakes, and stone fly patterns provided continuos action.

Be careful when you flatten your hook in catch-and-release waters, as I lost a trophy Rainbow from a broken hook that I possibly put too much pressure on when creating a barbless hook! Broadacres stocks barbless hook flies in all patterns.

Above: *The lodge cabins are warm, comfortable, and luxurious, right down to the goose-down beds and comforters. A full kitchen provides a "cook your own" cuisine, or a ten-minute trip to the old tavern or hotel in Creede will warm your insides with delicious food. Broadacres is all about clean mountain air, luxurious accommodations in log cabins, and trophy wild trout surrounded by the romance of the late 1800s.*

Broadacres is a complete hospitality destination. Architects are currently working on a beautiful new main lodge and dining room, scheduled for completion in the fall of 2003. Nearby Creede is most assuredly part of this destination experience, as it dates back to the silver boom of 1892, with Bat Masterson and all of the old flavor of a ghost town that is still alive with 400-plus inhabitants and scores of little shops and galleries to investigate.

Above: *The Rio Grande is truly one of North America's pristine fisheries. After a brief morning shower (complete with a magnificent rainbow in the sky), we experienced a caddis hatch resulting in numerous rainbow and brown trout. Their color and stamina bear testimony to a great fishery of clean, cold water and an abundance of bug life for nutrition.*

Right: *Cutthroat, browns, and rainbows all rose to our dry flies in the month of June. We used droppers with bead-head nymphs (Copper Johns and Princes) in the midafternoon when the water temperature rose from 55 to 62 degrees.*

Our fly selection consisted of Pale Morning Duns, Blue Quills, Caddis, and Parachute Adams. Stone Fly patterns are a must to have on hand for the numerous stone fly

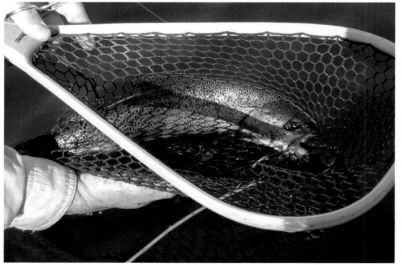

Above: *The landscape along the Rio Grande is generally open and favors wide-open fly casting.*

Left: *The office and main entrance to Broadacres.*

Above: *Shallow Creek is Broadacres' best-kept secret, teeming with trophy rainbows and browns. It is a pristine spring-fed creek that provides opportunities to sight-cast and stalk the big ones.*

Right: *A Broadacres guide helps anglers read stream conditions.*

Opposite page: *Another nice "hook up" on the Rio Grande. Broadacres covers approximately two and a half miles of the headwater in the Rio Grande fishery. Catch-and-release techniques with barbless hooks protect the fish and provide a more sporting approach to fly fishing for all anglers.*

Broadacres Ranch is fly fishing at its best, with all the comforts of home and plenty to do for non-anglers (so bring the family). A blended combination of the magnificent outdoors, the rich history of the west, and a fly fishing experience extraordinaire! April through mid-October will provide the novice, intermediate, and experienced angler with all he or she can handle . . . including some awesome caddis and stone fly hatches on the Rio Grande and Shallow Creek.

THE HIGH LONESOME
LODGE

Colorado's
High Mountain Country

Rose and Buzz Cox know exactly what you need and what you are looking for, and they provide everything and more when you visit High Lonesome Lodge. Originally from Northern Maine, the couple add a lifetime of camp organization and fly-fishing adventure to the rugged mountains on the western slope of the Rockies.

High Lonesome Lodge has exclusive rights to vast acreage, featuring a spring-fed creek that has been designed by man and nature as one of the great Colorado fisheries. The resident beaver, having dammed up over eighty pools of pristine fishery water, changes the fishing experience as each pool differs from the 5,000-foot elevations to the cooler 7,500-foot elevations! Water temperature plays an important role in the feeding habits of trout.

When you come to High Lonesome Lodge, be prepared for big fish, Aunt Linda's homemade "everything," and a wonderful outdoor experience in the high mountain air of Colorado's western slope.

Rose and Buzz Cox

Right: *Beautiful trophy-size brook trout are one of the many species in the fisheries at High Lonesome Lodge. Brett Mouser of Denver, Colorado, nets a beautiful rainbow at the Upper Reservoir Hole.*

Cutthroat, browns, and rainbows all rise to dry flies in the month of June. But in mid-June begins a exciting phenomenon peculiar to the topography of High Lonesome: an extended hopper hatch that continues into the summer as the temperatures gradually change up the mountain. Natural formations and beaver dams forma series of some eighty ponds on the still water spring creek from 5,000 to 7,200 feet in elevation. The hoppers start to hatch at the lowest elevations, then, as the summer season progresses and water temperature rises at increasing elevations, new hatches occur farther and farther up the mountain in a stairstep effect that lasts well into July. At High Lonesome we found that droppers with bead-head nymphs, in midafternoon when the water temperature rises from 60 to about 68 degrees, would produce some really big fish. Reliable fly selections of Pale Morning Duns, Blue Quills, Caddis, and Parachute Adams are the main patterns.

Left: *A beautiful 24 inch rainbow caught on a hopper at mid-morning during an awesome "hopper hatch"*

Below*: Joney's Pond is one of the High Lonesome Lodge trophy fisheries, providing browns, rainbows and an occasional cutthroat. The beavers keep the water levels high and the water is filled with an abundance of bug life.*

High Lonesome Lodge

The main lodge is centrally located 150 yards from the guest lodge. A short morning walk in the delicious, clean mountain air will ready your appetite for the early morning breakfast, served in the main dining room. High Lonesome's kitchen staff is known for down-to-earth home cooking (you will want seconds) - which will surprise you with everything from eggs Benedict to Aunt Linda's Tex-Mex and homemade pies! They also provide wonderful "stream lunches," not to mention the outdoor barbecue and country music on occasion.

Above: *The guest lodge consists of a game room and a spacious living room for guests to mingle at the end of the day. The comfortable bedding complete with hand-crafted quilts for a wonderful night's rest are welcomed details to complete the facilities. It accommodates a maximum of twelve guests.*

Opposite top: *The High Lonesome Lodge entrance to office and fly shop*

Opposite bottom: *The main dining room, complete with all of the wonderful "fixins" of good country cooking*

Opposiote top: *At the end of a great day it is a "must" to take a short ride to visit the "Goblins." One of nature's odd rock formations almost come to life in the early evening hours.*

Opposite bottom and above: *High Lonesome Lodge is a canvas of beauty. Fishing for trophy trout in this landscape of continuous beauty, will provide you with a truly wonderful experience on the western slopes of the Great Rocky Mountains.*

THE HIGH LONESOME LODGE

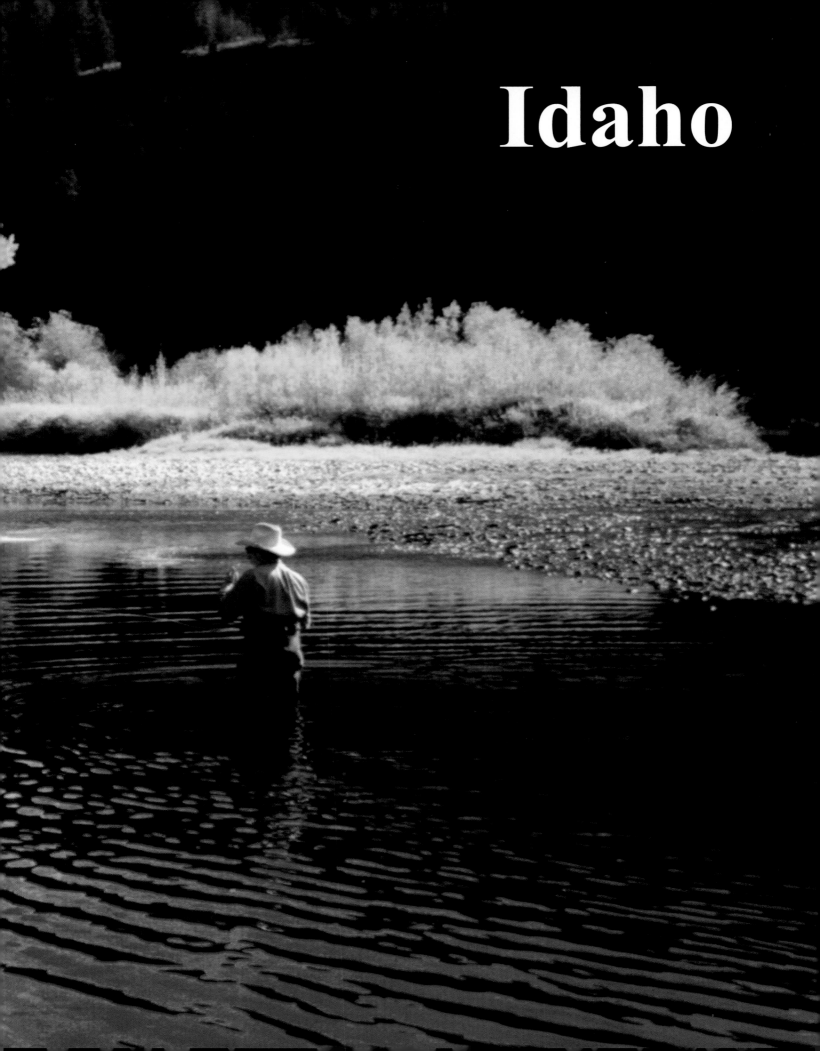

Idaho

Lonnie's son, Mitch, fishes the falls just outside the park in this magnificent Idaho setting.

Three Rivers Ranch

Idaho

Montana

Yellowstone National Park

Wyoming

Thee Rivers Ranch

Robinson Creek

Before the Lord rested on the seventh day, he created Three Rivers Ranch in Idaho. Three Rivers Ranch is located on Robinson Creek in the heart of Idaho's finest wild rainbow, cutthroat, and brown trout fishing. Ideally located in eastern Idaho, just minutes from Yellowstone National Park and the Grand Tetons, its honor roll of wild fisheries includes many famous rivers in addition to special places like Railroad Ranch and Box Canyon. The fishing is legendary, and the huge choice of fabulous waters is the "angling heart" of this old, established fishing ranch.

Lonnie Allen is the third-generation owner. Her grandparents, Fred and Berta Lewies, acquired the property. Her parents, Harry and Lillian Lewies, added to the ranch and protected it for future generations. They all created a special oasis in the world of fly fishing. When Lonnie's father, Harry, said his final goodbyes, he remarked, "Well, I guess I've thrown my last Renegade" (a dry fly). I believe Harry is still throwing that Renegade down old Robinson Creek and the other historic waters of Idaho in the twilight hours of each day if you just take time to look for him in the shadows!

Special destinations emanate from the spirit of the special people who maintain and create them. The Indians say, " It matters not where the body lies, for it is like the grass . . . where the spirit dwells, that is where you want to be."

Early one evening, after fishing on the South Fork of the Snake River, I slipped on my waders for a second time, rigged up my 4-wt. rod and line, and stepped down into Robinson Creek to quietly enjoy what Harry meant about walking this stream. In the quiet evening pools, rainbow rose to Harry's worn-out Renegade, and I again experienced the essence of "time in the stream." Harry possessed this knowledge and passed it on to his daughter Lonnie and to everyone he touched. I tried to describe this spirit to myself, and an old-timer gave me the simple answer: "He was the type of spirit you just wanted to be with." Harry passed it on to Lonnie, all the wonderful family members, and the staff of Three Rivers . . . and it's still there. All I wanted to do that evening was just be there, throwing that old Renegade!

Top: *The rustic lodge and great room come alive each morning and evening with expectations of the day to come and the tales of "how it got away" during the evening cocktail hour.*

Above: *Lonnie Allen represents third-generation ownership and also loves fly fishing. The dynasty continues with Lonnie's son Mitch who guides at Three Rivers.*

Right: *A view of Robinson Creek looking across to the original homestead of Fred and Berta Lewies. Today it is a guest cabin.*

Doug Gibson, head guide at Three Rivers Ranch knows where the rainbows hangout!

Above: The Teton River is best fished with a MacKenzie-style drift boat, one guide and a maximum of two anglers. Get ready for some action. The guide will place you on the runs and holes with occasional wading in this beautiful freestone stream.

One of the really great fly-fishing guides in North America, Doug Gibson, also throws that old Renegade fly that Harry loved so much. Doug also ties a bunch of special patterns almost guaranteed to arouse even the toughest fish. Having fished and guided for over thirty years at Three Rivers Ranch, he is an icon for what fly fishing is all about: a dedicated angler, a masterful guide, and above all, a good friend. Add to all of this that Doug can tie a fly faster that you can throw a line. He's never without a good hand-tied fly and a good story to go with it. Guests actually plan their trips according to when Doug can take them fishing! We spent a great day together fishing some very special places, including a secret spot in Yellowstone Park. The camaraderie was icing on the cake. I learned a few new tricks . . . old dogs *can* still learn. My name is already on the waiting list to fish with Doug when I return to Three Rivers. When I asked Doug to talk a little about himself, he replied, "Well . . . I'll let you do the horn blowin'!" Doug doesn't do much talking about himself but when it comes to fly fishing, he can sure fire put you on fish and tell you some great fishing stories about the old-timers . . . and it comes straight from the heart.

Doug will be at Three Rivers Ranch for as long as the grass grows. It's all located in Warm River, Idaho, and it is just that . . . *warm*! Warm hospitality, lots of good home cooking, wonderful people and fisheries that just won't quit. And don't forget to join old Harry down in Robinson Creek if you ever get there it's just a few steps off your cabin porch into a small stream filled with rising rainbows (actually just a few seconds off your cabin porch into heaven).

Lonnie's son Mitch guided me down the Teton on the first day of my visit. I was immediately submersed into the fly-fishing experience of Eastern Idaho as we navigated the majestic Teton river in the MacKenzie-style drift boat. These boats are ideal for comfort, angling freedom, and transportation to each of the runs and pools. Mitch tied on a hopper pattern to arouse the local residents. Seconds later, a big cutthroat came on to finish that fly's life! It was a slow, rolling take. I had to be patient for a second before setting the hook. He was on and he was mad. He did the "cutthroat roll," an over-and-over roll in the water designed to shake the hook free. Mitch advised me to lower the rod tip, providing a reduction in pressure, and when the rolling was finished, put him back on the rod with full pressure. Many times anglers fail to play the fish with the rod alone - the reel is only for taking up the slack. My 4-wt. rod and 4-wt. clear line were responding to the challenge. Mitch called for a little more slack for the barrel rolls, and I again stripped back for a tight line.

I moved the cutthroat across the bow into slower water and attempted to move the fish from the faster water where he had the advantage. He rose again, heading for the middle of the tail-out. This strategy was effective in using every bit of the fast current in his attempt to break free. I moved him once again into the slower water applying steady pressure on the line. This was a great battle, which I was winning inch by inch. On light tippet and the under weighted rod, the experience kicked up a notch. I thought the fish was exhausted, but suddenly he exploded into the air as Mitch lowered the net into the water. The result was cutthroat 1, angler 0. With a final lunge over the net, the hook pulled free. But zero disappointment was registered on either side. The final outcome of numerous battles changed many times during the morning hours. After a delicious stream lunch on a nearby sandbar, we renewed our attack with a #14 hook that presented an unseen pattern from British Columbia: a green fuzzy body with a red belly band in the middle (top water fly) finished with a white tuff tail. Mitch was astonished as it dominated the day! It is always interesting to try a completely different pattern from the accustomed presentation in each fishery we visited. To my delight, this one became the champion of the day.

Opposite: *One of the many healthy and beautiful trout of the Three River Ranch fisheries. Three Rivers boasts over a dozen major streams, forks and fisheries that will keep you busy for a couple of years!*

Left:: *An angler displays the unusual pepper-like pattern found on the Teton River cutthroats.*

Below: *Many of the important assets of Idaho fly-fishing are the uncrowded streams and fisheries where you can still spend a day in the outdoors and be one with nature.*

Right: *Guide Mitch Allen helps a Three Rivers angler net another fine catch on the North Fork of the Snake River.*

Below: *This rainbow was caught on Harry's favorite fly, the Renegade. The dry-fly action of the Idaho fisheries is one of the major attractions of fishing these pristine rivers and streams. Note that besides their brilliant coloring and length, these cutthroat and rainbows are well fed, with an ample bug life resulting in fat fish with a lot of girth. And this means action on a fly line!*

Left: *A stream lunch prepared by the staff at the lodge, is one of the favorite aspects of this fly-fishing adventure. Everything from a gourmet-style bacon, lettuce and tomato sandwich to a few home-baked desserts to help keep your energy level up for the remainder of the afternoon.*

Below: *The clear, freestone streams allow for numerous wading opportunities. Idaho's best kept secret is the healthy and tough physical condition of their trout. It's a pure delight to get out of the drift boat and spend some quiet minutes wading an inviting run or tail out for those "lunkers."*

Maine

Above: *The Spring Hole at River Camp. Maine's wild flowers accent the stunning beauty of the North Maine Woods.*

Right: *Matt provides floatplane transportation to all of the remote spots and destinations. Libby has ten remote camps on lakes and streams in addition to the main camp. Evening flyouts after an early dinner to remote lakes, landing on a two-foot-deep gravel bar and waiting for the evening green drake hatches, are memories that will last a lifetime.*

Libby Sporting Camps

Millinocket Lake is located within the 3.5 million acres of the North Maine Woods. Here, in a time forgotten habitat of glacier-formed lakes and heavy wooded forest, you will find one of the great traditional trout lodges dating back to 1890. Matt and Ellen Libby continue the Libby Camp tradition, providing a once-in-a-lifetime adventure in fly fishing.

It is a continuation of family tradition and pride founded by Matt's grandfather, great-uncle, and great-grandfather. Today it remains a wild country of woods and water, abundant in wildlife. Beaver, black bear, moose, deer, waterfowl, and eagles dwell along the streams and lakes that are the home of the most beautiful brook trout and landlocked salmon in North America.

We arrived in late June, which was the beginning of the most sought after hatch in fly fishing; the Green Drake Hatch. A modest 1-1/2 hour flight from Boston to Presques Isle, Maine (29 miles from the central northern border to Canada) provides easy access to the region. Matt Libby picked us up in his four-passenger float plane at Hansen Lake, less than fifteen minutes from downtown Presque Isle (pop. 10,100+) Matt's floatplane was to be our sole transportation to the fisheries of northern Maine. We arrived at the lodge on Millinocket Lake, twenty minutes later. As soon as we landed the warm rustic old lodge, with glossy yellow logs, hard pine floors, moose rack chandeliers and mounted wildlife trophies, all welcomed our stay in this backwoods castle of fly fishing.

Above: *The comfortable and rustic cabins of the Libby Camps are a visit into the days of old. Each cabin has an old stove for the crisp nights and the propane gas lighting system is simple and efficient.*

Directly after dinner our first day, Matt took me by motor boat then by Indian canoe to Ellen's Pool, just above Round Pond. We fished in a misty light rain, hoping in vain for an evening hatch. We hooked up three healthy brook trout before darkness overcame our valiant efforts. Walking back from Round Pond in the dark, we filled our lungs with the sweet smell of balsam Christmas trees and listened to the quiet peace of the forthcoming night. We arrived back at the lodge about forty-five minutes after sunset with all the comforts of home. I slept like a bear in winter.

The next morning I visited two of the out camps, Spring Hole Camp and River Camp. My guide, Joe Christianson, threw everything but his fly box at the River Camp Hole in my pursuit of an old trophy salmon that was seen on numerous prior occasions. After an hour and a half of continuous and persistent fly selection, Joe tied on a size 16 Parachute Adams (old mainstay) on my 5-wt. rod. With a single cast into the shade of a tail-out bubble stream under a huge tree, we saw him rise and engulf the fly. I set the barbless hook softly as the water exploded with his energy.

I prefer a tip-flex rod, (more accuracy is obtained with a tip-flex) and this old warrior quickly gave it a sound testing! Rod and fish were an even match. The importance of waiting for him to tire without overplaying his runs from one direction to the other was the key to landing this beauty. He was eighteen-plus inches and jumped out of the net after removal of the Parachute Adams from his jaw.

After a delicious stream lunch of king-size sandwiches ranging from ham and cheese to pastrami piled a mile high, we hiked in the stream 1/4 mile to the Spring Hole. Once again after some experimentation and lack of any top-water action, we changed to a Black Wooley Bugger, which netted three nice brook trout and of course "missed the big one" when the line pulled out.

As we rounded each bend in the Aroostook stream, I felt as if I could visualize two huge men with safari brim hats: ghosts of Teddy Roosevelt and Jack Dempsey, side by side in the stream, enjoying the pristine waters of this beautiful mountain environment. It was their favorite place to relax and enjoy this great sport of fly fishing. I was enjoying walking in their footsteps.

Above and below: *The lodge-dining hall and kitchen (recently remodeled) all date back to the early years of Libby Camps and many of the artifacts have been preserved to retain the romance and history of the camp.*

Above: *The many animals that represent the wildlife surrounding the lodge.*

Opposite: *The huge dining room and large rock fireplace are the center of the lodge activity. When the dinner bell clangs about ten times, you are being summoned to a gourmet of country cooking.*

Opposite insert: *Ellen Libby makes just about everything you can imagine from scratch, including wonderful home -baked bread and jams and desserts to please a king.*

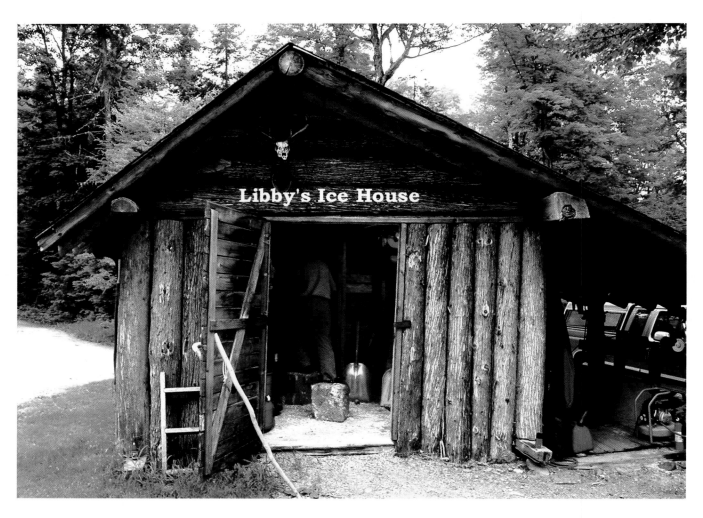

Covered with sawdust   **Sawdust hosed**   **Finished**

Above: *Each winter, Libby Camp cuts over 40,000 pounds of ice by chainsaw when Millinocket Lake freezes over three feet thick. It is then sledded to the old Libby icehouse. Packing snow between the blocks of ice as it is stacked provides a cushion for storage. Covering it with sawdust and a tarp will then secure the icehouse for the entire year and season to come.*

Many folks have never seen an icehouse, let alone taken out a block of ice, washed it off with water and chipped away chunks with an ice pick for their icebox or cooler. It's just everyday life at Libby Sporting Camps.

Above: *Beautiful brook trout lie in quiet glacier lakes and streams accessible only by floatplane. After an hour's hike with a light backpack, you have paid the price to fish in waters that will provide a morning and afternoon of unequaled angling pleasure.*

Left: *A canoe can be sometimes confining for long stretches, and we found that fly-fishing float tubes not only provided easy access but were effortless to use. Water-foot fins provided all of the propulsion required to fish and navigate the entire lake.*

Above: *One of the many streams that Libby Camps fish for the ultimate in brook-trout fishing. These beautiful, serene streams, glacier lakes, and remote woods and forests provide a total experience in fly fishing in the great outdoors of Maine.*

Left: *The purple Iris is native to norther Maine.*

Opposite top: *This remote outlying camp, one of ten beside the eight cabins located by the main lodge, is fully equipped, providing comfortable accommodations. Each cabin, a miniature of the beautiful main lodge, is hand-built and crafted by the Libby family from the pine and spruce fir logs so abundant in the surrounding forest. An old wood-burning stove, a modern kitchen, hand-quilted blankets, and wonderful bedding are all part of the Libby experience.*

Opposite Insert: *Libby guide Mike Langley caught this 20-inch brook trout on the last cast of the 2001 season.*

"Moments in the Stream
The Pere Marquette River, Michigan

Fly Fishing
North America

Michigan

Painting depicts Father Marquette arriving at St. Ignace in the Straits of Mackinac.

Jorgensons

RR Bridge Hole

Gleasons Landing

Swag Hole

Tree Run

Old Reliable

Geezer's Bend

4th Clay Bank

3rd Clay Bank

Swing Hole

Waddell Riffles

Sand Hole

Danaher Creek

Burnt Cottag

Pere Marquette River

Map: *The map shows the fly water from M-37 down to Gleason's Landing, with reference to many fishing holes. The Pere Marquette is a "Blue Ribbon Trout Stream" and one of the ten best trout rivers in the United States.*

The fishing river area is 20 to 40 feet wide, with a mix of sand and gravel bottom. Its depth ranges from one to six feet, making for easy wading from drift boats that provide full access to the stream. Access: Forks Landing, M-37 Bridge, Green Cottage, Gleason's Landing, Boman's Bridge, Rainbow Rapids, Upper Branch Bridge, Walhalla Bridge, Indian Bridge, and Custer Bridge.

Pere Marquette Lodge
(PM Lodge)

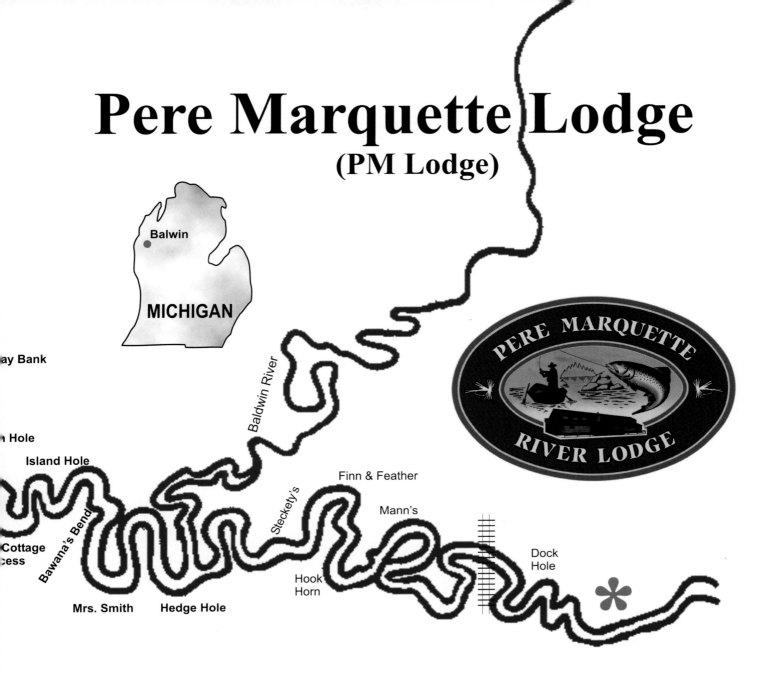

Many authors and writers have captured the history and geography of the Pere Marquette River. It winds for sixty-seven miles to Lake Michigan, passing through Baldwin, home of the rustic Pere Marquette Lodge. The main lodge features cabins on the stream and a central lodge where anglers can gather each evening for cocktails and camaraderie. Meals are available in the lodge dining room, or in nearby Baldwin for those who seek local flavor. The old fireplace in the lodge can tell many a tale about presidents Herbert Hoover and Teddy Roosevelt fishing the stream, in addition to the adventures of Ernest Hemingway (who considered the river one of his favorite steelhead streams)and many other dedicated fly fisherman.

The Pere Marquette is the only river in North America to be known by its initials, "PM." The French priest Pere (Father) Marquette loved the river, which was named for him after his death in 1675 by the local Indians (who called it the River of the Black Robe). Grayling, now almost extinct in America, flourished in abundance on the PM but then vanished after the logging boom in the late 1800s ruined the ecology of the stream. Due to the demographics of this historic fishery, however, the river proved indestructible.

A closer look into the water reveals the fish stacked up in this section of the Pere Marquette fly water.

Above: *An early morning start on the Pere Marquette in one of the typical MacKenzie-style drift boats*

Early Morning Start
for Steelheads

The gin-clear water of the PM is a product of the numerous springs that create this awesome fishery. Ideal soil conditions absorb excessive rains and protect the PM from flooding. The soil actually acts as an additional filter in maintaining clarity. Now add the natural hydraulics of numerous pools, runs, and holding water to complete a complex but simple recipe for a "Blue Ribbon Trout Stream." The numerous bends and curves are short and narrow. Imagine catching a really big, powerful fish in a very small area - and you have the heart of the Pere Marquette Lodge fishery.

The PM River, the PM Lodge guides, and the diversity and quality of the species quite possibly make this lodge untouchable when we consider the top fisheries in North America.

Lodge owner Peter Yoon is a dedicated fly fisherman and a retired chemist. His focus is modernizing the lodge to twenty-first-century standards while retaining the rustic, old-world charm of this famous fishing lodge. He was helpful in explaining the history and romance of the Pere Marquette Lodge and placed a great deal of emphasis on his PM guides.

Guides are as important to the PM experience, as is the reliability of your equipment. Consider six professional year-round guides! Because the PM can be fished year-round, the top guides in North America are attracted to its waters; more fishing time, more trophy species, and the beauty of this stream are equally rewarding to both guide and angler. The PM has been covered numerous times *in National Geographic* and other magazines.

The MacKenzie-style drift boats are like New York taxicabs to the next fishing spot. After drifting a short distance, you exit the boat and stand in shallow water. In most cases you will be fishing to a specific target pointed out by the experienced guide. You are now fishing to a trophy fish in a narrow and pristine forest fishery and about to experience a huge explosion in the water. That's serious fly fishing!

With this brief history and stream description, we turn our attention to the trophies. In late October, the fall steelhead, referred to as "silvers," "chromers," and "metals," begin to run. They are fresh-run fish from Lake Michigan. To Northern Michigan fishing guides, this is the moment they wait for each year. These fish are the hardest fighting fish in North America! They feed aggressively this time of year on salmon eggs (compliments of the annual spawning cycle) from the huge chinook salmon run which begins in late August and finishes up in the early weeks of October. It's comparable to a huge smorgasbord in the stream.

Late autumn and fall provide numerous fishing opportunities for browns, salmon, and steelheads. The Michigan coho salmon and lake-run browns become very active before winter, working their way up to spawn. The steelheads hold over in the stream and continue to feed during the winter, waiting to join up with the massive runs coming in to spawn in the spring. Nice browns are caught throughout the winter along with the steels.

Below Right: *Laura and Tom Pollack of Colorado with a fresh run female steelhead*

Below left: *Sam Cefaratti Jr., Chicago, is eleven-years old and did not want anyone helping him catch his first steelhead. Sam caught this thirteen pound steelhead with a P. M. Wiggler (fly) in the Sand Hole on the lower flies only zone.*

Bottom: *Pere Marquette senior guide Walt Grau, has been guiding for the PM lodge since 1989. Walt displays one of the fresh run steelheads caught by one of his guests.*

As spring warms into summer, big streamers are used for the wild browns. As the water continues to warm, the browns become reckless, crashing bait fish into the banks. Prolific hatches of Hendricksons, sulphurs, and gray drakes begin the May fly season. Then it begins to snow at night with the *Hexagenia lambata* hatches. This is huge trophy brown trout time, with an occasional Skamanian (summer steelhead). That's right, summer steelheads!

As summer unwinds, a great terrestrial season explodes with hoppers, ants, and beetles! Catching big trout in the middle of the day will melt this fishery into your heart forever. Keep your eye open for that big king salmon. They arrive in August and begin the cycle once again. And let's not forget the brook trout in the headwater of the PM, with blazing yellow, red and orange bellies.

I often marvel at God's calendar of events. When you consider a salmon returns four years later to where it was bred, busting full of eggs with only one chance to get it right, lays her eggs, and then dies; it's a remarkable journey without a road map and zero practice!

My favorite time to fish the PM is the fall run of the steelheads. Ten-pound average steels will send your reel screaming with an explosion of energy unequaled in the spring runs.

We fished the fly-water section of the PM from M-37 to Gleason's Landing. The beauty of the late October colors were second only to the three beautiful "chromers" we hooked up (all before lunch!). Eight-wt. rods with a 10-wt. line allowed us the ease of roll-casting into the runs and pools.

My heart pounded with each strike as I took on the challenge of each battle. Veteran angler Fred Steuber was our guide that day and was instrumental in landing these trophies. Steelhead fisherman know what a steelhead can do and my second strike was a classic example. She hit hard, sending my reel into flames, and my rod looked like a willow tree branch. The steelhead remained motionless for a brief moment. Suddenly the fish made a run straight at

Coauthor Lou Perella with
a 14 pound Chinook salmon

my rod, breaking water and thrashing the air for freedom. The line tangled on the rod tip. Without experience, I lowered my tip to the water, a runout by the fish took it off, and we again renewed an awesome battle. Barrel rolls, runs, attempts to gain fast-water advantage, runs at logs, and numerous aerials are but a few of the maneuvers I enjoyed. Motionless holding patterns of deception - you perceive she is tiring, and then comes a sudden burst of energy. After twenty minutes, I moved her to the bank out of the fast water. Within a foot of the net on two successive occasions, she jumped out of reach and renewed the struggle.

I had played my first strike of the morning for about the same amount of time when, disappointingly, the line broke. I yelled over to Fred, "I don't know how much more this line will hold." I feared a break-off at any moment. The steel continued the fight, and I moved her once more in front of my guide to allow him to net the fish from behind. Somehow she saw the net coming again and moved out right where Fred had anticipated the fish would go. He scooped in this beauty and I yelled, "Good job, Fred what a beautiful fish!" "You played her perfectly," he responded and whether I did or not was not important. This steel was landed! My heart continued to pound as he put her on the "boga" (a great fish tool for gripping the fish without premature release). She weighted eleven and a quarter pounds, and of course we started taking pictures.

PM guide Fred Steuber and Coauthor David Mouser
with a 11 pound fresh run steelhead

Steelheads in the PM River are real heart-pounders. You want to catch a really big fish in a small stream? No problem. Magnificent forest setting, clear water, shallow wading, and drift-boat transportation on the Pere Marquette is my recommendation. We fished for four days, and I only wish it had been longer.

The guides cooked a hot stream lunch on their gas porta-grills. Steaks, shish kebab, barbecue, and pork loins, are standard. Their lunches are out of this world.

The Pere Marquette River is a very special place in North America because it's an unplanted fishery. The fish are wild, and their beauty is self-evident from their bright silver to their deep browns and reds. Their wild leaps out of the water are magnificent.

(Special thanks to PM guide Jeff Hubbard as contributing author)

Head guide Jeff Hubbard with an 18 pound steelhead

Above: *PM Lodge guide Tommy Lynch with a ten pound fresh run winter steelhead*
Right: *Owner Peter Yoon with an eighteen pound fall run steelhead. Both fish were caught in the "fly only" waters between M-37 and Gleason's Landing*

Left: *PM Lodge guide Steve Warfield with PM guest Bill Kidder*
Below:: *The natural beauty of the Pere Marquette and the solitude of the stream remains the same today as when Father Pere Marquette first discovered it over 350 years ago.*

P. S.   In 1914 a law was proposed in the Michigan legislature to allow spear-fishing of steelhead in the Pere Marquette due to the massive number of fish in the fall and spring runs.

Montana

Big Horn River Resort

Bighorn River Resort is the "gentleman's resort" of fly-fishing destinations, just one and a half hours by automobile from Billings, Montana. It overlooks the Bighorn River in the valley of the Bighorn in Fort Smith, Montana. Seven individual cabins overlook the river. From the back deck of the main lodge you can see the famous "Aquarium Hole."

The main lodge is elegant, spacious, and warm. The upstairs loft and veranda host evening cocktails just before dinner, as guests share their many stories of the day's adventures.

Francine Forrester holds court in the dining room, with gourmet dishes that you will die for each evening. Hint: Don't turn down the fruit medley with a hint of fresh mint, mangoes, grapes, blueberries, and something secret to make it an unforgettable delight. My personal favorite was breakfast with eggs Benedict.

;Above: *Guests find quiet time in the main lodge.*

Far left: *Lodge dining room*

Left: *Upstairs loft where evening cocktails are amplified by stories of the day*

Opposite page: *Main lodge, cabins and bedroom.*

Under the direction of Nick Forrester, lifelong friend Beau Devereux is the man who makes things run. Besides his duties, Beau is the head fishing guide (when requested or needed). The day's activities begin with the guide parings. Beau is acutely aware of each guest's ability and personality. Each guide is matched to best complement the guest's angling skills.

Fly fishing the Bighorn River is by drift boat, with numerous shallow-wading opportunities throughout the river's course. Many anglers are well aware of the names: the Drum, the Probe, the Landing Strip, the Suck Hole, the Aquarium, the Car Hole, the Meat Hole, the Tree Hole, the Five-Dollar Hole, Grey's Cliff. The rainbow and brown fishing is possibly the finest in North America. The icy cold water temperature of 45 degrees is a result of the release of water from the bottom of the Bighorn Reservoir, which provides an excellent fishery for big rainbow and brown trout. The average catch is twenty per day, and the size averages 16 inches with larger trophies at 22 to 26 inches! And I must add that these fish are "pigs" - they are long and they are very fat, and your rod will certainly bend to not only their weight but to their fight.

Top:: *Getting the drift boats and the gear ready for the morning fly runs is the first order of business. Beau Devereux rigs up the starting fly patterns.*

Above: *Looking across to the Aquarium Hole.*

Left: *This beautiful rainbow trout is typical of the healthy and fat conditions of the fish in the Bighorn. This is about the average size for the Bighorn River (nothing but fatties).*

Forrester's
Destinations

Above: *The Landing Strip is one of the great wading holes on the Bighorn.*

Right: *Bighorn guests Guy Hollingbury and Carol Swayne enjoy one of the fabulous stream lunches prepared for each guest as they break for some midday nourishment. A cool, gentle breeze, a delicious lunch complete with linen and gourmet delights thanks to Francine, and a stage to enjoy it on . . . the Bighorn River.*

Top left: *One of the beautiful Bighorn browns lurking in the shadows along the banks.* Top right: *The Bighorn is noted for trophy rainbows and plenty of them.* Above: *Drifting the Bighorn in a MacKenzie-style drift boat is the normal method of fishing the river with numerous areas to anchor or get out and wade if you choose.*

I was surprised the first morning when Beau Devereux, Bighorn River Resort guide, introduced me to a #20 size hook and fly patterns such as a Black Caddis, a Sow Bug, a Ray Charles, and a Flashback Pheasant Tail. Beau was my fishing guide during my stay at Bighorn River Resort. I was excited to get started after the stories of big fish and lots of them!

We started below the dam in a Mackenzie-style drift boat using a Double Dropper Nymph with a float indicator. The bug life on the river is abundant, but early in the morning the water temperature is too cold for hatches, so we began with a Ray Charles and a Sow Bug. Within ten minutes my float indicator submerged. I lifted for the set, and shortly thereafter we netted the first of about twenty-four fish. This first one was a beautiful, wild 16-inch (fatty) rainbowand he had a lot to say about being caught. The Bighorn fish are eager to fight, and if you are looking for action you don't have to wait long.

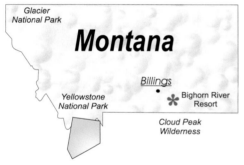

Top: *These magnificent browns and rainbows speak for themselves.   Bighorn River Resort guests Bill Berta and Craig Battisfore show one of the many rainbows they caught on dry flies. Guide Dale Davidson (left) was kept busy with the net.*

Right: *Head guide Beau Devereux lands a beautiful brown trout for a Bighorn angler. It was taken on a dry-fly hopper pattern in the Landing Strip Hole.*

Above: *Trophy size beautiful Bighorn River rainbow*

We netted over twenty rainbow and brown trout averaging 16 to 19 inches in a combination effort of floating downstream in the drift boat and wading where the fish were stacked up.

The highlight of my day was late morning as the water warmed. We changed to dry flies as the surface began to gently boil with rising trout. Beau tied on a # 20 Black Caddis on both our rods (I insisted he join me). His second cast to a "rise ring" was an 18-inch big-belly rainbow, dancing in midair, fighting for freedom at any price. Before long the fish was in the net and ready for pictures.

As Beau released the rainbow, he motioned to a rise about twenty-five feet at two o' clock. I missed with two shots as the wind pushed my line about eight feet to the side, just right of target. He rose again and I quickly picked the line up off the water and shot it six feet left of the splash. I had the correct distance. The wind pushed it into the target area. *Bam!* He hit it solid in the lower jaw. Another 18-inch beauty was bending my 4-wt. rod to the max. Beau netted him after about ten minutes and we decided to call it a draw, netting two nice 18-inch rainbows.

As the sun set that first day, I did not want to quit but my body told me at was time to call it "quits." The landscape was pristine and magnificent to behold. I could almost see General George Armstrong Custer riding with the 7th Calvary along the bank in route to his last battle just a short distance away with the Sioux Indians. I looked at Beau and said, " If George would have just taken up fly fishing instead of guns, he'd probably have stayed here awhile and lived to tell a few Bighorn River fish stories!"

Drift boats provide comfortable access to the stream

Look closely at the rock ledge in the center of this picture to see the "spirit face" (two eyes and nose) in this sacred fishing hole of the Sioux Indians *(located on the South Fork known as "Indian Rock")*

Spotted Bear Ranch

Montana's Spotted Bear Ranch

Would you like to be one person in a million population or one person in a thousand acres? High up in the Flathead National Forest, in the northwest corner of Montana adjacent to the Glacier National Park and the Bob Marshall Wilderness, you may have your wish (one person in a thousand acres). It is a two-hour drive from the Kalispell airport to the doorstep of Montana's wilderness. What a place!

Owner Kirk Gentry is the "cowboy" behind this remote and beautiful environment. This part of the country is loaded with bear, moose, elk, and wild creatures called "cutthroat" that readily answer to a dry fly, especially in July and August . Twenty to twenty-five fish a day are not unusual, and there's plenty of fight to go along with the action.

Fred Haney is the head ramrod for Kirk, and the minute he welcomes you to the lodge, it's time to get your rod and put on your gear. Just a hundred yards from the main lodge is the South Fork of the famous Flathead river, Montana's most beautiful freestone, clearwater stream.

We arrived (my son Brett joined the adventure as cameraman) in mid-September, the tail of the season. The number of fish caught each day went down, but the size went up! In addition, we enjoyed Montana's beautiful fall colors of crimson and yellow that were bursting out all over. Primary access was by raft; two anglers per boat with one guide was standard. Rods were 4-wt. and 5-wt. (your choice), and the patterns were Caddis, Royal Humpys, Renegades, and Royal Wolffs. We tied a Prince Nymph on as a dropper and used the same rig with a Copper John (about 14 inches down from the dry fly). All of the action was dry-fly on top. An angler's dream!

Once the "ammunition" was established, we proceeded to raise 14- and 15-inch wild West Slope cutthroats that were a lot of fight and hard to land. These fish are sensitive to heavy tippet in September, and we moved to a very light 7x tippet with 7x leader for effectiveness. Veteran guide Dan Dowd, an experienced fly fishing guide of thirteen years, taught us a lot about the influence of weather, wind, clouds, air temperature, and stream conditions. This increased our level of appreciation. Everything Dan said came true right down to where the fish were located and what would be the best pattern to use. The scenery, the solitude, and the remoteness are the key elements to Spotted Bear Ranch and the enjoyment of Montana's remote wilderness. If you are looking for that end-of-the-road experience in the great outdoors, the state is Montana and the place is Spotted Bear Ranch.

The ranch has clean and comfortable rustic log cabins complete with fireplaces (the temperature gets chilly sometimes during the night high in the mountains). The food is down-home country style vittles with an ample supply of delicious homemade desserts. The South Fork is twenty miles of beautifully clear, cold, clean water teeming with trout runs throughout Spotted Bear Ranch. It is truly a remote wilderness experience, "Where the Adventure Begins!" The terrain is a solid carpet of mountainous forest, abundant in wildlife and Montana's rugged landscape features, all adjoining the famous Bob Marshall Wilderness. Spotted Bear provides backpacking on horseback into the Bob Marshall and, for the ultimate fly-fishing adventure, you can experience Montana as Lewis and Clark first saw it. While fishing awesome trout waters, it would be a sin not to take time to enjoy the magnificent scenery at every bend the river.

We floated the lower South Fork our first day and the upper South Fork the second day. The water was 52 degrees in the morning hours, rising to 59 degrees by afternoon. The runs, holes, and tail-outs are as numerous as the stars. Prior to our third day, we experienced the proverbial Montana weather change. A drop in the barometric pressure and some rain in the evening hours dictated the approach to fishing the next morning.

We waited until 11:30 a.m. Twelve hours of lower pressure was enough time to stabilize the fish. After the fish got used to the change in pressure, they would begin feeding again. Dan remarked, "They still have to eat, but the standard patterns will probably have to change." Sure enough, he was right. Dan advised us to choose a pattern completely opposite from what we had used the preceding day. What worked then would not usually work under the present weather conditions. I tied on a Black Caddis pattern with a red tuft tail. The first cast was a 15-inch golden-back cutthroat. The pattern quickly died, and I then tied on a Black Stonefly pattern. Again, one cast and another beautiful cutthroat with a quick decay to any further rise. Brett tied on a Mayfly pattern. Another quick rise and take was followed by complete refusals on further casts. Three beautiful Montana cutthroats averaging 16 inches in size were our reward. After thirty to thirty-five minutes of action the wind came up and, with it another weather change. That was it. Dan said we might as well be thankful for what we enjoyed, and with an hour of "zero rise" we decided to call it a day as the weather continued to roller-coaster in on us.

We certainly enjoyed a great stream lunch, three really nice rises to three completely opposite patterns, and another great day of fishing. Sometimes it's the quality and not the quantity. I often wonder what I enjoy the most just being in the stream, or the action and rise to the fly. There is a special quality associated with both. Once on, the fight is important, and it's always good to be able to release a fish. If he wins and the line goes limp, it's still great! After all, it's the total time you spend that makes it all worthwhile.

Opposite page: *The South Fork of the Flat Head river*

Top: *Main lodge*

Top inset: *Individual cabins*

Above Right: *Lodge great room*

Above Left: *Lodge dining room*

Right: *Enjoy a buckboard ride after dinner.*

Top left: *Entrance to Spotted Bear Ranch*

Left: *Getting ready to push off down stream*

Bottom: *Typical cutthroat on the South Fork river*

Montana

Top: *Cold mountain springs provide the icy-cold water necessary to support the West Slope cutthroat.*

Above: *Spotted Bear guide Dan Dowd picks up a nice cutthroat on the upper South Fork.*

Right: *Brett Mouser, from Denver, caught this beauty on a Yellow Humphy.*

(Above) Owner Kirk Gentry
"This is Where *The Adventure Begins* "

One of the most challenging streams in Montana.

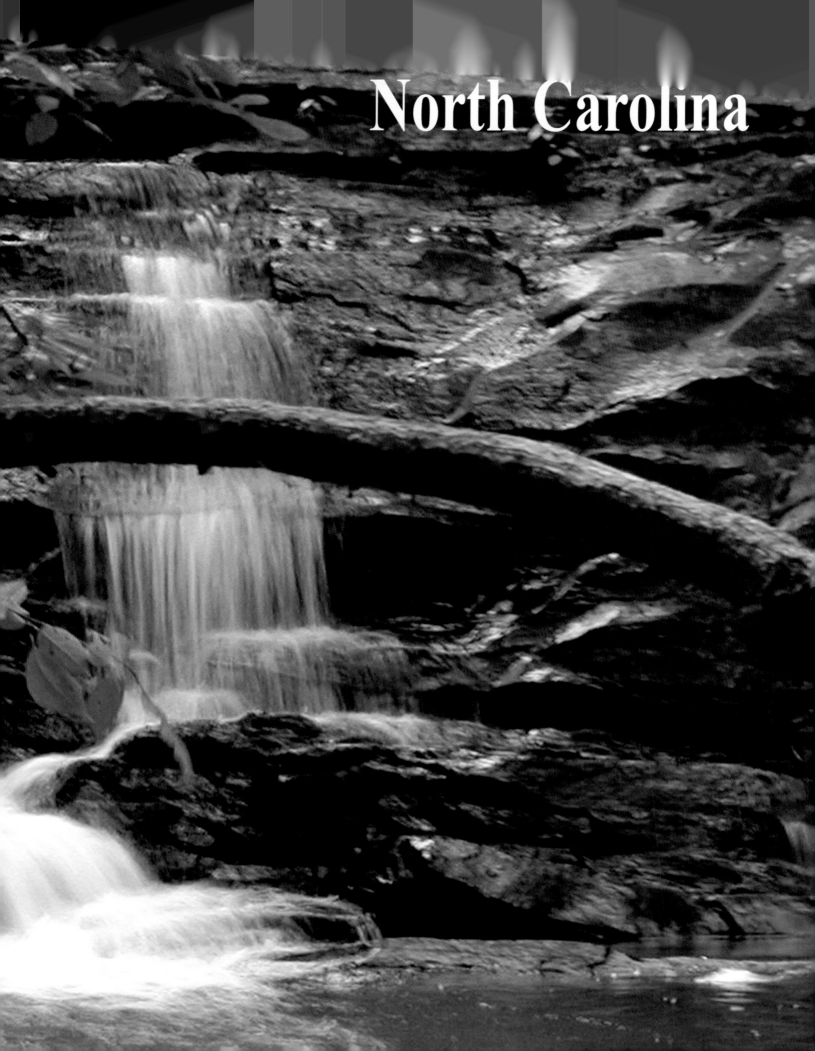

North Carolina

The "Heartland" of Fly Fishing

Many of the old-time fly fishermen believe that the heartland of trout fishing lies in the Appalachian Mountains that cover five states. The "capital city" of this area is Asheville, North Carolina. Every spring, thousands of beginner, intermediate, and experienced fly enthusiasts flock like pigeons to the beautiful and pristine cold mountain streams of North Carolina. While resorts and lodges that provide the ultimate in fly fishing are few and far between, it's here in northwestern North Carolina that we find an abundance of fly-fishing activity.

With over 2,000 miles of streams supporting populations of trout, the "top ten" list of trout fisheries in northwestern North Carolina includes some real gems. Rivers large enough to float and fish are few; they include the Tuckasegee River, the Catawba River, and the Toe River. Just to the north, the Tennessee Valley Authority (TVA) has created some spectacular tail-water fisheries accessible for float trips by local guides. Small-to-mid-sized freestone streams are the rule, following steeply graded courses through mountains covered in rhododendron, laurel, dogwood, hemlock, and oak forests. The triple-canopy forest covering this convergence of mountain ranges (the Great Smokies, the Southern Appalachians, and the Blue Ridge Mountains meet in the vicinity of Asheville) provides the shade cover necessary to keep streams cold enough to support trout in such southern latitudes. Notable among these freestone streams are the Davidson River and the South Toe River (managed as fly-fishing only, catch-and-release waters); the streams of the Pigeon River watershed above Canton, North Carolina; the Wilson Creek watershed below Boone, North Carolina; the Nantahala River and its tributaries; and the Snowbird Creek and Santeetlah River watersheds in the far western portion of the state. The Great Smoky Mountains National Park, which straddles the border of North Carolina and Tennessee, offers another 2,000 miles of flowing trout water, with legendary streams such as Big Creek, Hazel Creek, Cataloochee Creek and its tributaries, the Oconaluftee River in North Carolina's boundaries, Abrams Creek, and the Little River drainage representing Tennessee on the western slope of the park.

The trout streams of North Carolina offer year-round fishing. While hatchery-supported trout streams are closed for stocking in March, streams managed for wild trout remain open to anglers all year. The peak of the season is from early April through mid-July, when the aquatic insects are most active. There is, however, a "second season" of excellent fishing available in the fall. As streams begin to cool in the mountain air of late September, trout (particularly brown trout) begin feeding with a purpose. That purpose is to load up on protein in preparation for spawning through the following month of October. This big event makes for great fishing during a time of year when the trout streams are deserted except for the dedicated few who are wise to the drama about to unfold below the surface.

Primary insect hatches that should be targeted in the peak spring season are the blue quill, quill Gordon, little black caddis, and March brown emergences in March and early April, followed by Hendricksons, mottled brown/gray caddis and blue wing olives in mid-April to early May. The month of May produces an explosion of insects on the streams: Cahills, sulphurs, yellow sallies (the ubiquitous yellow stonefly provides great fishing during its extended hatch, May through June), the giant Potomanthus mayflies and, for a grand finale (approximately Memorial Day weekend), the Eastern green drake hatch. This famous hatch, which occurs (at different times) as far north as Maine, is much sought after by anglers throughout the East Coast for the size of the bug and the tendency for large, cannibalistic trout to rise eagerly to the evening spinner fall (better-known as the Coffin fly, after an imitation of the insect developed and popularized by the famed New England flytier Harry Darbee).

The off-peak seasons also offer hatch-matching opportunities, with terrestrial insects such as ants, beetles, and inchworms becoming important to the trout as the aquatic insect activity winds down. The inchworm is an especially effective pattern throughout late May, all of June, and early July. The dog days of August and early September offer a wonderful opportunity for a change of pace to the angler: smallmouth bass. As trout streams warm and trout fishing slows, the conditions improve on the lower-elevation streams that harbor good populations of these feisty fish, and fly fishermen can find plenty to amuse themselves while they await the cooling days of October and a return to the trout streams.

120

Big Butte Lodge

Top: *Big Butte Fishing Camp and Lodge*

Above left:: *The lodge living room*

Above right: *Entrance to the kitchen*

Right: *Simple and rustic lodge bedroom*

Opposite page: *Dining and kitchen*

122

A very special and secluded fishing lodge provides the basics for learning to fly fish in North Carolina. Big Butte fishing camp, on the Big East Fork of the Pigeon River, was purchased in early 1990 by several partners from Asheville, North Carolina. Big Butte has about 3/4 of a mile of frontage on the Big East Fork (its upstream boundary adjoins the Pisgah National Forest), several ponds, and a view across the valley toward the now famous Cold Mountain.

Big Butte's lodge is a beautiful, rustic log-cabin complex dating back to 1810. Charles Frazier's best-selling novel *Cold Mountain* clearly describes this outdoor paradise. The mountain looks down on one of the old log cabins, which many believe is the same one Frazier's characters visited in the winter of 1865 as they fled the aftermath of the Civil War. The log beams in the main lodge are over thirteen inches thick. The property at one time belonged to Dr. Logan Robertson, a physician from Asheville, whose great respect for the rustic nature of the place and its few original structures is evidenced in the restorative enhancements he made as he developed the lodge for use as rehabilitative quarters for his patients.

Today Big Butte offers schools tailored for large or small groups of mixed company, women-only, and private weekends of instruction for individuals and families. In our opinion, it is one of the premier "fly schools" in North America. Frank Smith and Drake Whitlock, owners of Hunter Banks Company (a unique fly shop and guide hangout) in Asheville, have put together a unique fishing camp. The lodge and its outbuildings can accommodate up to twenty-two people. Fully equipped kitchens allow guests to cook for themselves, although full-chef services are available upon request. Guide services are available for fly-fishing guests. The stream is well managed as a result of the programs implemented by the local Trout Unlimited chapter. It is designated as a semi-private fishing preserve.

The Big East Fork of the Pigeon River (running through the property) provides the on-site experience of learning to fish in a stream, while Big Butte Lake provides a well-stocked "fish laboratory" of one-, two-, and three-pound rainbows for anglers to test their skills after learning the basics. It is here that coauthor Louis Perella learned, in early May, the fundamentals of fly fishing to prepare for our forthcoming adventures.

The entire lodge is rustic and holds an ancient charm. For the intermediate or experienced angler, Big Butte is a wonderful place to sharpen your skills. No matter what your experience level, you can learn something new, or easily correct bad habits. The rainbow-stocked lake is especially important. We used it as a testing ground for new flies and a laboratory environment to view the habits of trout as they feed both topwater and underwater.

We affectionately like to refer to Big Butte as "fly fishing school." It is 100% a rustic, outdoor stream and lake experience dedicated to nothing but angling. And the camaraderie we shared during our stay here rivaled that of any remote lodge destination we visited.

Over the years we have attracted a number of friends to the world of fly fishing. We urge you to take time to visit Big Butte for a couple of days, take some new "inductees," and enjoy a wonderful visit to the stream! We assure you it is a very rewarding and educational outing.

Above: *Coauthor Lou Perella fishing among the Rhododendrons and the Hemlock-lined banks of the Big East Fork of the Pigeon River in the higher elevations of the Appalachian Mountains for brook trout.*

Right: *Casting upstream to drift the bubble stream and work the tail out water behind a large boulder where brook trout are feeding in the shade areas.*

Asheville   **North Carolina**   ● Raleigh

*
Big Butte
Fish Camp

● Charolette

BIG BUTTE LODGE - NORTH CAROLINA

124

 # Moments in the Stream

Fly fishing is not complex or difficult to enjoy or understand. The rules are simple. Put on some waders, tie an artificial fly on the end of a line, then shoot the line out in an ever-increasing arc and allow it to rest gently on the surface of the water. It is the art of deception. Presenting an artificial fly to a hungry trout and hoping he mistakes it for a meal is the essence of the sport. When the water explodes and the fish struggles to free his mouth from the steel hook that disguised itself as a succulent morsel of food, you will then understand the excitement of fly fishing. Your rod bends from his strength and the line spins off the reel as he makes his run. Time almost stands still during this encounter. He will either free himself or become your unwilling captive for a brief moment. If you are skillful enough to land him, you will enjoy the thrill of success! This experience provides a one-on-one competition between men and women - young and old - and a wild trout. It holds other special moments that will come and go like a gentle breeze against your face.

Fly fishing can fold time and cause hours to become minutes. Time spent in a stream can bond people together even if they never meet again. Around the bend you may tip your hat or exchange a warm greeting that extends beyond the brief moment of strangers meeting for the first time.

When I made my first visit to New Zealand in the fall of 2001, I was alone early one morning fishing for trophy rainbows. In front of me, moved a beautiful, crystal-clear stream with a smoke-like gray mist hanging just above the water. A tall native New Zealander (obvious by his style of clothing) stepped into the water directly across from me on the other side. He motioned to me with a nod of his head and said, "Morning, mate!" I smiled and replied, "Good morning, sir." We fished together in silence as time stood still. We both hooked up some beautiful four- and five-pound rainbows (I must mention these are the average weight for the Tongaraio River on the North Island; they will spoil you) and after tidying up our gear to venture on, he addressed me for the second time. "Good to see you Americans still traveling, mate!" (referring to the drop in airline travel post-9/11). I responded, "Thanks for leaving a few of these nice rainbows in your streams for us to enjoy!" Hearing my reply, he nodded silently to me, then turned and walked away. We only spoke twice to each other that morning, but as we parted, we separated as friends.

Our kinship at that moment was bonded in the stream - simple exchanges between two strangers who did not know one another but yet did. I sometimes wonder if we placed all of the world leaders in the middle of a trout stream and left them alone for a few days, if the conflicts in the world would cease to exist.

Friendship is a special value that must always be earned. Ever wonder when and where our most trusted friends come from? Mostly our youth - when we had nothing to hide from one another - a time of simplicity and trust.

Fly fishing, in many ways, emulates those magical moments from our youth. Special moments bonded in the stream among friends and even strangers will bend time and render it motionless.

A warm exchange of words and gestures, the result of a mutual passion to throw a simple line across the water hoping to deceive a wild trout for a few brief moments, created a special moment in the stream. A moment in time, ever so brief, searching always for that instant when we look for a big fish to rise, was our bond. Water runs through the stream like teardrops from a thousand stars, and time disappears in their reflection as I become one with myself. I cherish each moment in the stream . . . I live for moments!

David Mouser
Coauthor

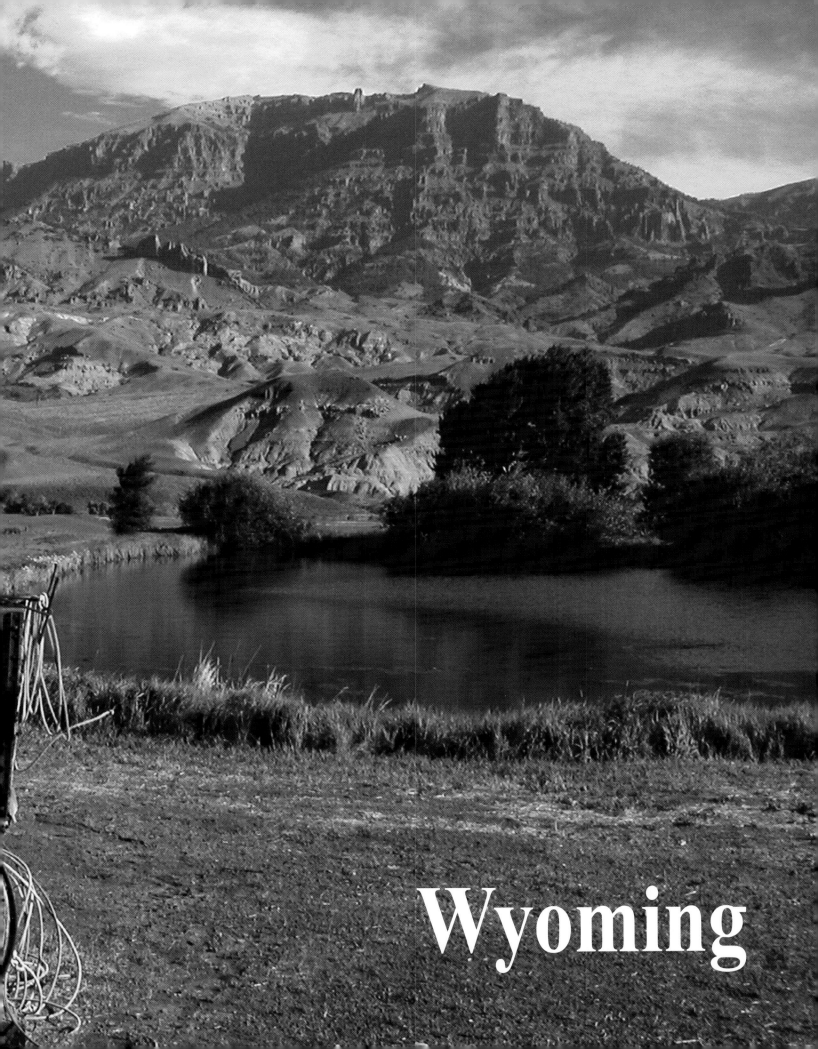

Wyoming

DNR Ranch (formerly Old Hollister Mansion) January 1906, Cody, Wyoming. Diary: *"Henry banked dirt around the bunk house, Lee delivered 3 head of cattle to N. E. Brown and measured 4-1/2 tons of hay from J. E. Jackson. Henry cut cottonwood. Weather very cold."*

DNR Ranch, August 2002, Cody, Wyoming. Diary: *"Perella Family arrived, Lou and Scott went fly fishing on the North Fork, a.m., Robin and Hilary rode north side of creek, a.m. Everyone went to Yellowstone Park, p.m. Huge campfire after dinner. Weather clear and mild."*

Welcome to the Old West and a fly-fishing adventure with lots of family involvement centered around a passion for wildlife. DNR Ranch is a trip back into the heritage of Wyoming and a very special family adventure on fabulous streams with your son or daughter (moms welcome).

The legend of the Hollister Mansion and the Hollister Ghost is a story right out of the Old West. It dates back to the original owners of the place, Dwight and Elizabeth Hollister. Dwight was diagnosed with cancer and, experiencing overwhelming bodily pain, he decided to take matters into his own hands. He dressed up in his Sunday suit, sat in his favorite reading chair in the main room, opened his Bible to his favorite passage, and then shot himself in the head (the bullet hole in the library wall is still visible). Dwight was a moonshiner by trade, and that sideline is what kept the ranch going, in addition to its function as a halfway stop for riders. Buffalo Bill Cody would stay overnight on his way to his hunting camp at Pashaska, as it was a day's ride to DNR from Cody and another day's ride to Monaco, his camp. Dwight and Elizabeth would provide feed and water in addition to a good meal and a night's lodging. After Dwight died, Elizabeth drank up the rest of the moonshine that was stashed thereabouts and became an alcoholic. After having too much to drink one evening, she accidentally drowned in the bathtub (which is still there in the mansion). There are many who testify to still seeing Elizabeth walking the floors at night. Oddly enough, she only shows herself to men and to women with blond hair (like Elizabeth's).

Opposite Page: *Hollister Mansion (DNR Ranch Lodge)*

Above: *Main dining room and original fireplace that warmed many a traveler, among them Buffalo Bill Cody*

Left: *The living room of one of the comfortable cabins located on the ranch. Cabins are complete with full kitchens.*

DNR Ranch is a place where you come as friends and leave as family. Ric and Dollie Horst are just plain "down home people with a lot of country spirit." They enthusiastically share their home, the magnificent Wyoming outdoors, and a fly-fishing ranch experience that is oriented towards family. Located 23 miles west of Cody and about the same distance from Yellowstone National Park, it is an easy hour-and-a-half flight from Denver on the regional airline carrier.

Above: *Frank Angelo, noted fly-fishing instructor and experienced guide, is waiting for you to go fly fishing at DNR Ranch. Over forty years of experience and a lifetime devoted to teaching beginners, novices, and advanced anglers is DNR's legacy to fly fishing in the historic rivers of the Madison, the Yellowstone, the Fire Hole, the Clark, and the Shoshone.*

Frank has taught thousands of dads and family members the easy steps to begin fly fishing. You will be fly fishing in minutes and wondering why you didn't try it years ago. For advanced anglers, a trip to the stream with Frank is a pure delight.

Frank is a staff member of prestigious fly-fishing companies in today's market and is a recognized instructor and seminar speaker. He continues his lifelong journey and dedication to fly fishing during the winter months from his home retreat in the central mountains of Pennsylvania.

For the new angler, he has created a simplified instructional video, *Fun with Fly Fishing: Beginning Your Journey.* DNR Ranch is proud to have Frank Angelo teach the sport of fly fishing to their beginners and experienced anglers . . . you are in for a fly fishing adventure with one of the greatest fly fishermen on the stream today! Frank is a pure delight to be with, and I guarantee you he will put a smile in any fly angler's heart in addition to ensuring a memorable adventure in the stream.

Names like the Dollie Hole, Devils Elbow, Chimney Rock, and the Big Rock Hole will become adventures in fly fishing when you fish the Shoshone River. The North Fork and South Fork of the Shoshone River are among America's best-kept secrets for wild rainbow and cutthroat fly fishing. Wildlife is abundant, and it is not uncommon for you to occasionally find a few bears fishing in the streams with you.

DNR offers a remote horseback fly-fishing adventure high in the mountains surrounding Yellowstone National Park. The horse ranch not only leads trail rides for family members, but, with advance notice, they will outfit a fly fishing trip complete with a base camp for overnight adventures into the high mountain regions. The higher elevations hold secret mountain lakes and fisheries that include the almost nonexistent golden trout.

Top: *North Fork of the Shoshone river*

Above left: *DNR provides trail horses for the mountain fly-fishing adventures*

Above right: *View of the mountains from your cabin*

Wyoming's best kept secret - The Shoshone!

Above: *Waiting for a rise on the North Fork of the Shoshone River just outside Yellowstone National Park. The waters of the Shoshone are fed by mountain snow runoff and numerous springs, providing an excellent water temperature for the cutthroat and rainbow habitat.*

Frank Angelo took me to the Dollie Hole late one afternoon to see if we could raise a couple of nice trout. We raised more than a couple before we called it quits.

We began with a dry-fly pattern for top water with a dropper of choice attached to the hook of a dry fly. I prefer to use a Royal Wolff, but this day but instead chose a hybrid Royal Wolff with rubber legs and a large yellow tuft on the top! It was sort of a stonefly pattern, yet truly something put together for fun. It floated well in the fast run, and with a Copper John for a dropper, I was ready for action.

An icy cold mountain creek empties into the Dollie Hole, creating a twenty- foot run with a nice long tail-out. We both enjoyed 14- to 16-inch rainbows and cutthroats until we noticed a caddis hatch coming off about 5:45 p.m. Frank changed to a caddis pattern and was catching some nice fish on a Prince Nymph dropper below the caddis. I changed to the same pattern.

We tied them about eighteen inches from the top, and by 6:30 p.m. we were reluctant to leave this secret hole. I made one last cast, and before my fly could touch the surface a wild cutthroat rose in midair and grabbed it. We looked at each other in amazement! The intensity of feeding trout seemed to be increasing with every minute. Needless to say, this fish was the trophy of the day. He fought to stay in the current and was a lot smarter than I realized.

Just when it seemed I had him turned, he had the strength to head back into the fast water to gain advantage. Once back in the current he would fight harder to free the hook. I promise you that at this point it is prudent for any angler to be patient. Let the rod tip do the work, and you will win more than you lose at this point. So many times after a strong battle, if the hook is not firmly set in the jaw, the line suddenly pulls free and the fish escapes. I gently worked him out of the current, letting the rod do the work. Frank quickly netted the handsome 18-inch cutthroat. And by the way, patience paid off as within seconds after capture, my fly pulled free from his lip. If I had applied line pressure to bring him out of the current, he would have won the battle. I always try to remember that the reel is for taking up the slack and the rod is for playing the fish. Simple rules in fly fishing can always make a difference.

Above: *DNR Ranch owners Ric and Dollie Horst land a nice rainbow on the North Fork of the Shoshone River at the Dollie Hole. Ric guides the more seasoned anglers into the secret holes and runs that are private water*

The Firehole flows gently through Yellowstone

DNR is dry-fly fishing at its best, with internationally renowned guide and fly instructor Frank Angelo. Here in the heart of the Old West, the beginner or experienced angler can fish while his family enjoys horseback riding, whitewater rafting, nights around the campfire with everyone sharing their stories of the day. And of course, the ghost of Elizabeth Hollister comes alive for a few moments. DNR is a very special destination centered around fly-fishing and the great outdoors for the entire family (and, by the way, don't forget Yellowstone National Park). The Yellowstone, the Madison, the Gibbons, the Fire Hole, the North and South Fork of the Clark, and the North and South Forks of the Shoshone are fabulous waters to fish. DNR Ranch can take your family there by horse or buggy!

DNR Ranch August 2002, Cody, Wyoming. Diary: "*Last day at ranch. We all went horseback riding after breakfast. Scott and I went fly fishing together - p.m.! I always wondered what it was like to fly fish . . . it's easy and it's a blast! We all were cowboys and part of the Old West for a few moments . . . and we did it as a family. Robin and Hilary joined us in the afternoon down on the stream and I believe they may be fly fishing with us next time.*"

Above: *The Shoshone flows gently along just outside Yellowstone Park*

Epilogue

We hope you have enjoyed *Fly Fishing North America* as much as we enjoyed writing it. We were just a couple of guys who went fly fishing to see the continent. I had never fly fished before, and David had forty years of experience. It was a learning adventure for both of us.

We wish to thank all of the destinations that provided warm hospitality and gave us the experiences of a lifetime. We were often asked by the guests that we encountered the following two questions: How did you pick each destination, and which one is your favorite?

Having obtained a list of destinations from travel sources and suppliers, we called each destination and researched the lodge and the fishery, and of course we diversified the geography. We believe we chose well, as there was never a disappointment. As for our favorite, each one became a favorite. Each location was very special regarding the geography and the fisheries. And each lodge was unique. The best answer to this question is simply: we will return to fish each one as soon as we possibly can! All were wonderful adventures. The lodge owners and guides are possibly the most important element. Without them, each destination would not have been special.

As a special note to the beginners who are motivated to try this sport after reading our book, I recommend learning from a professional. Make sure your first few visits to the stream are with a guide. Even though David had fished for more than forty years, he directed me to Drake Whitlock in North Carolina (one-on-one at Big Butte) for a two-day school that gave me the confidence that I could fish anywhere. By the way, 60% of the guests at the lodges we visited were beginners when they arrived (but not when they left)!

Please feel free to visit our web site. We welcome your comments and suggestions, beginners and anglers alike.

Louis Perella

Louis Perella
Coauthor

www.flyfishingnorthamerica.com

**Fly Fishing
North America**